In Support of
Arab Democracy:
Why and How

In Support of Arab Democracy: Why and How

Report of an Independent Task Force

Sponsored by the Council on Foreign Relations

Founded in 1921, the Council on Foreign Relations is an independent, national membership organization and a nonpartisan center for scholars dedicated to producing and disseminating ideas so that individual and corporate members, as well as policymakers, journalists, students, and interested citizens in the United States and other countries, can better understand the world and the foreign policy choices facing the United States and other governments. The Council does this by convening meetings; conducting a wide-ranging Studies program; publishing *Foreign Affairs*, the preeminent journal covering international affairs and U.S. foreign policy; maintaining a diverse membership; sponsoring Independent Task Forces; and providing up-to-date information about the world and U.S. foreign policy on the Council's website, www.cfr.org.

THE COUNCIL TAKES NO INSTITUTIONAL POSITION ON POLICY ISSUES AND HAS NO AFFILIATION WITH THE U.S. GOVERNMENT. ALL STATEMENTS OF FACT AND EXPRESSIONS OF OPINION CONTAINED IN ITS PUBLICA-TIONS ARE THE SOLE RESPONSIBILITY OF THE AUTHOR OR AUTHORS.

The Council will sponsor an Independent Task Force when (1) an issue of current and critical importance to U.S. foreign policy arises, and (2) it seems that a group diverse in backgrounds and perspectives may, nonetheless, be able to reach a meaningful consensus on a policy through private and nonpartisan deliberations. Typically, a Task Force meets between two and five times over a brief period to ensure the relevance of its work.

Upon reaching a conclusion, a Task Force issues a report, and the Council publishes its text and posts it on the Council website. Task Force reports reflect a strong and meaningful policy consensus, with Task Force members endorsing the general policy thrust and judgments reached by the group, though not necessarily every finding and recommendation. Task Force members who join the consensus may submit additional or dissenting views, which are included in the final report. "Chairman's Reports" are signed by Task Force chairs only and are usually preceded or followed by full Task Force reports. Upon reaching a conclusion, a Task Force may also ask individuals who were not members of the Task Force to associate themselves with the Task Force report to enhance its impact. All Task Force reports "benchmark" their findings against current administration policy in order to make explicit areas of agreement and disagreement. The Task Force is solely responsible for its report. The Council takes no institutional position.

For further information about the Council or this Task Force, please write to the Council on Foreign Relations, 58 East 68th Street, New York, NY 10021, or call the Director of Communications at 212-434-9400. Visit our website at www.cfr.org.

Task Force Co-Chairs

Madeleine K. Albright

Madeleine K. Albright

Vin Weber

Vin Weber

Project Director

Steven A. Cook

Steven A. Cook

Task Force Members

Feisal Abdul Rauf

Khaled M. Abou El Fadl

Odeh F. Aburdene*

Madeleine K. Albright

Nancy Birdsall

Daniel M. Brumberg

Leslie Campbell

Steven A. Cook

Larry J. Diamond

Michele D. Dunne*

Noah Feldman

F. Gregory Gause III*

Amy W. Hawthorne

Robert J. Katz

Mel Levine

Abdeslam E. Maghraoui

Joshua Muravchik

Michael N. Pocalyko*

William A. Rugh*

Anita Sharma

George Vradenburg III

Vin Weber

Tamara Cofman Wittes

Tarik M. Yousef

*The individual has endorsed the report and submitted an additional or a dissenting view.

Arab Interlocutors

Cairo, Egypt
January 26–28, 2005

Fahd bin Abdullah
al-Mubarak
Malaz Financial Advisory
Saudi Arabia

Ahmad E. Bishara
National Democratic Movement
Kuwait

Rola Dashti
Kuwait Economic Society
Kuwait

Abdel Raouf El Reedy
Mubarak Public Library
Egypt

Munira Fakhro
University of Bahrain
Bahrain

Mustafa B. Hamarneh
University of Jordan
Jordan

Osama al-Ghazali Harb
Al-Siyassa Al-Dawliya
Egypt

Taher S. Helmy
American Chamber of Commerce
Egypt

Sa'eda Kilani
Arab Archives Institute
Jordan

Habib C. Malik
Lebanese American University
Lebanon

Hala Mustafa
al-Dimoqratiya
Egypt

Abdulaziz Sager
Gulf Research Center
United Arab Emirates

Note: The Arab interlocutors from the Cairo consultations are not responsible for the content of this report. They participated in their individual and not institutional capacities.

Contents

Foreword

Over the past five decades, U.S. policy in the Arab world has been predicated largely on the notion that the political status quo in the region best served Washington's interests. With the assistance of Arab partners such as Egypt, Saudi Arabia, Jordan, Bahrain, Kuwait, and Morocco, the United States built a remarkably good record of achieving its objectives—notably, protecting the free flow of oil from the Persian Gulf, ensuring Israel's security, confronting rogue states, battling terrorism, and during the Cold War, containing Soviet influence in the region. Yet the terrorist attacks on New York and Washington, DC, on September 11, 2001, challenged the underlying assumption of U.S. Middle East policy. Within a short time after the attacks, policymakers began to question whether authoritarian political systems in the Middle East were sources of stability or the primary causes of the political alienation and extremism that fueled organizations like al-Qaeda. The Bush administration clearly believes the best way to "drain the swamp" that produces terrorists is to promote democracy and reform more broadly in the Middle East.

The Council on Foreign Relations established this Independent Task Force to consider whether promoting democracy in the Middle East is in the best interests of the United States and, if so, how Washington should implement such a policy. The Task Force reached the conclusion that, notwithstanding short-term risks, democracy in the Middle East is a desirable goal. In its report, the Task Force asserts that over the long run, the development of democratic institutions in Arab countries "will diminish the appeal of extremism and terrorism, the risks of revolutionary upheaval, and the emergence of regimes openly hostile to the United States." From these important findings this Task Force report offers a comprehensive set of policy recommendations for the Bush administration to promote an "environment in the Middle East that is conducive to peaceful democratic change."

The Council is deeply appreciative of two eminent public servants, former Secretary of State Madeleine K. Albright and former Representative Vin Weber (R–MN), for chairing this effort. Their intellectual leadership steered the Task Force toward consensus on an issue of significant importance to the United States and the Arab world. My thanks also go to Steven A. Cook, a next generation fellow at the Council who specializes in Arab politics, who skillfully directed this project from its beginning. Finally, I wish to thank the Task Force members for this important contribution to the national debate.

Richard N. Haass
President
Council on Foreign Relations
June 2005

Acknowledgments

The Independent Task Force on U.S. Policy toward Reform in the Arab World is grateful for the leadership of the co-chairs, Madeleine K. Albright and Vin Weber. Their intellectual leadership, broad experience, and bipartisan spirit were the invaluable foundations upon which this project was developed.

From September 2004 to February 2005, Task Force members and observers participated in seven meetings held at the Council on Foreign Relations in Washington, DC, and New York, as well as at the offices of Monticello Capital in Reston, Virginia. This diverse group of regional specialists, business leaders, foreign policy practitioners, and representatives of nongovernmental organizations (NGOs) brought unrivalled expertise to the challenges and opportunities confronting the United States and the Arab world.

This Task Force benefited immensely from the input of a group of Arab interlocutors from across the region who spent three days with the co-chairs and me in Cairo in late January 2005. We appreciate their time and pointed critique on the substance of our report. We are also grateful to the Council's national members in Los Angeles, San Francisco, Boston, Atlanta, and Chicago for their helpful comments on various drafts of the report.

The co-chairs and I are grateful to Kareem Idriss, Task Force research associate, for his constant resourcefulness and energy, his deft diplomacy throughout our Cairo consultations, and his editorial and substantial contributions and close attention to Arab sensitivities throughout the drafting of this report. Special thanks to Lee Feinstein for his guidance throughout this entire project. Lindsay Workman provided generous support in handling a variety of tasks associated with this project and was an invaluable asset to the co-chairs and me during our trip to Cairo. Lindsey Iversen developed the Task Force website with the assistance of Cree Frappier and Tom Davey. Irina Faskianos and the Council's National Program were extraordinarily helpful in reaching out to the Council's national members in various cities.

Thanks to Patricia Dorff for her careful support in the editing and publishing stages of this report. Special thanks to Lisa Shields and the Council's Communications Department for their efforts with press activities during the report's rollout. I would also like to extend my gratitude to Jamie Smith, Diana Sierra, Suzy George, MargaretAnn Corbett, and Tyler Brown for their wonderful cooperation and support from the planning stage to completion of this report. Hassan Al-Ashhab did a great job of translating this entire report and Evan Langenhahn helped develop the appendixes.

All those involved in this project are grateful to Richard N. Haass, president of the Council, who presented the Task Force with its mandate and challenged the group to think critically in examining the issues at stake.

Finally, the Task Force would not have been possible without the financial support of Robert Belfer, the Ewing Marion Kauffman Foundation, Merrill Lynch & Co., Enzo Viscusi and ENI S.p.A., and Ezra Zilkha. We deeply appreciate their generosity.

Steven A. Cook
Project Director

Map of the Arab World

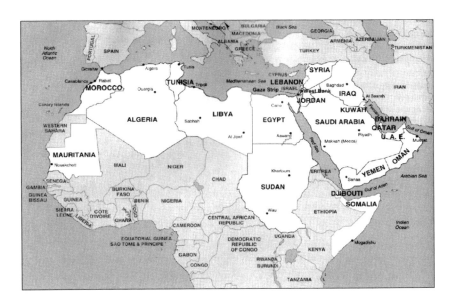

Courtesy of Arab American National Museum.

Task Force Report

Executive Summary

The Middle East will be a central focus of U.S. foreign policy for the next generation and beyond. While the list of challenges in the region is long, the Arab world also presents opportunities. In a region marked by a "democracy deficit" and limited economic prospects, there is also ferment. From Marrakesh to Cairo and Ramallah to Riyadh, Arabs are engaged in intense debate, self-reflection, and reassessment of their societies. Washington has a chance to help shape a more democratic Middle East. Whereas emphasis on stability was once the hallmark of U.S. Middle East policy, democracy and freedom have become a priority. Indeed, U.S. policymakers concluded shortly after the September 11 attacks that the prevailing domestic political, economic, and social conditions within Arab countries were a serious national security concern.

Through a critical examination of regional developments and an assessment of U.S. options, the Task Force sought to answer two primary questions: First, does a policy of promoting democracy in the Middle East serve U.S. interests and foreign policy goals? Second, if so, how should the United States implement such a policy, taking into account the full range of its interests?

The Task Force's answer to the first question is "yes." The United States should support democracy consistently and in all regions of the world. Although democracy entails certain inherent risks, the denial of freedom carries much more significant long-term dangers. If Arab citizens are able to express grievances freely and peacefully, they will

3

be less likely to turn to more extreme measures. They will also be more likely to build open and prosperous societies with respect for human rights and the rule of law.

In answer to the second question, the United States should promote the development of democratic institutions and practices over the long term, mindful that democracy cannot be imposed from the outside and that sudden, traumatic change is neither necessary nor desirable. America's goal in the Middle East should be to encourage democratic evolution, not revolution. Policymakers should take into account the region's political and economic diversity, its lack of a strong democratic tradition, and the challenge of moving beyond the relatively simple process of holding elections to the construction of independent and sustainable democracies. America's goal should be to support the development of democratic systems that are open to participation across the ideological spectrum, excluding only those who refuse to commit to peaceful procedures.

Findings and Recommendations

- Promoting political, economic, and social change in the Arab world requires a country-by-country strategy. Nevertheless, a number of basic principles should be emphasized across the region, including human rights, political representation, constitutional checks and balances, tolerance, rule of law, women's rights, and transparency of decision-making. Despite its recent emphasis on democracy in the Middle East, Washington has yet to speak in a consistent manner to various Arab countries on these important issues.

- The Bush administration should encourage Arab leaders to develop public, detailed "pathways to reform" that respond to the specific demands for change made by citizens within their countries. The public nature of these plans would help Arab citizens hold their leaders accountable to specific political, economic, and social benchmarks.

- This report is not about the Arab-Israeli conflict, but U.S. policy on that subject is relevant to America's credibility in the region. The Task Force believes the United States should continue its renewed diplomatic engagement to help ensure that Israel's withdrawal from the Gaza Strip proceeds smoothly and the two parties uphold their commitment to the "Roadmap for Peace." Washington's engagement will also help ameliorate Arab mistrust of U.S. intentions in the region. The United States should not accept the argument made by some Arab leaders that progress toward democracy is not possible until the Palestinian question is settled, nor should the United States accept the view espoused by some Israelis that peace negotiations should not resume until the Palestinian Authority is fully democratic. The United States should support democratic reform in the Middle East whether or not there is progress toward peace, as well as support progress toward peace whether or not there is significant democratic reform.

- For better or worse, Islamist movements and political parties are likely to play a prominent role in a more democratic Middle East. The United States must remain vigilant in opposing terrorist organizations. That being said, it should not allow Middle Eastern leaders to use national security as an excuse to suppress nonviolent Islamist organizations. Washington should support the political participation of any group or party committed to abide by the rules and norms of the democratic process. To reduce the possibility that Islamist movements will overwhelm more open Middle Eastern political systems, Washington should promote constitutional arrangements that would restrain the power of majorities to trample the rights of minorities. Most democracies have mechanisms such as an upper chamber of the legislature chosen on a specialized basis or a supreme court that guards against the "tyranny of the majority."

- Washington should promote economic and political reform simultaneously. All the available data indicate that economic growth is crucial for the durability of democracies but does not directly cause democracy. Favoring economic reform at the expense of political reform would ignore the democratic rights and political demands of Arab citizens.

- One of the most important factors hindering foreign direct investment in the Arab world is the fragmented and small size—in terms of capitalization—of the Middle Eastern market. Along with bilateral initiatives such as qualified industrial zones (QIZs), trade and investment framework agreements, bilateral investment treaties, and free trade agreements, Washington should provide assistance to improve regulatory environments, reform tax codes, and, most important, remove barriers to intraregional trade in an effort to promote regional economic integration.

- Corruption remains a significant impediment to Arab economic development. One of the surest ways to reduce corruption is through deregulation and greater integration with the international business community. With less regulation there are usually fewer opportunities for bureaucrats and others close to the state to demand kickbacks, payoffs, or commissions. As in other regions, greater integration with global businesses will allow Arab companies and entrepreneurs to gain access to capital based on what they do, not who they know. Another important instrument in the fight to control corruption would be the establishment of truly independent and resourceful counter-corruption commissions.

- The Task Force recognizes that there are problems with the way U.S. foreign policy is portrayed by Arab news networks and newspapers. While it is appropriate for Americans and U.S. policymakers to criticize what they regard as inaccurate and biased coverage on Arab satellite news networks, Washington's message about democracy and freedom is damaged when policymakers exert pressure on Arab governments to alter the content broadcast on these stations.

- Overall, the development of alternative Arab media outlets is a positive trend. The United States should promote the expansion of the private media market in the Middle East. A more democratic environment will provide Arab media consumers with more choice and better quality. Concomitant with Washington's push for privatization of Arab media should be an emphasis on improving laws that protect freedom of speech.

- The United States has done a poor job explaining its policies in the region and spreading its message about democracy and freedom. Washington's public diplomacy strategy needs to be changed. The

Voice of America's (VOA) Arabic service, which was previously the U.S. government's means of broadcasting news and information to the Arab world, should be funded once again and become an integral component of Washington's public diplomacy strategy, emphasizing reform issues in addition to news and information about the United States. Washington should also alter the content of its own Arabic satellite channel, al-Hurra. Because the channel is operated by the U.S. government, the suspicion is strong within the region that it is merely a conveyor of propaganda. To correct this, some of al-Hurra's programming should be shifted to a C-SPAN–style format. Broadcasting the practices of the United States and other democratic governments, including congressional and parliamentary hearings, political rallies, and debates, would expose Arabs to free political systems in action.

- Arab educational systems have generally done an inadequate job of preparing students for the global economy. Although Washington's involvement with Arab education reform is fraught with political and cultural hazards, the U.S. government should seek the partnership of Arab, American, European, and Asian educational institutions, foundations, the private sector, and multilateral organizations to develop teacher-training programs, provide technical assistance to decentralize Arab educational systems, help further expand English-language instruction, and help establish lifelong learning through adult education. Given Washington's goal of promoting economic and scientific development in the Middle East, Washington should also promote partnerships between U.S. business and engineering schools and Arab educational institutions.

- The prevailing visa policy of the United States is a significant barrier to worthy cultural, educational, and scientific exchanges. While recognizing the delicate balance the Department of Homeland Security must strike between protecting the country and maintaining its traditional openness to foreign students, Washington must improve procedures for allowing students from the Arab world to enter the United States.

- The Task Force believes that the policy and diplomatic components of the Middle East Partnership Initiative (MEPI) should remain within the State Department, but the bulk of MEPI's funds should be shifted to an outside independent organization such as the National Endowment for Democracy or a newly created Middle East foundation. Many Middle Eastern nongovernmental organizations (NGOs) are reluctant to accept direct transfers from an arm of the U.S. government.

- The United States currently provides approximately $5.5 billion annually in economic and military assistance to the Arab world, excluding reconstruction assistance for Iraq. As a general principle, the United States should use the promise of additional financial support as an incentive for reform. Although it has yet to dispense aid, the United States already has a program that would condition aid in this way to developing countries—mostly in Africa and Asia—called the Millennium Challenge Account (MCA). The funds will be distributed to those countries that have income per capita below a certain level (in 2005 below $1,465) and are best able to use them based on sixteen specific reform-related criteria, including accountability, rule of law, education reform, and economic freedom. Currently, only four Arab countries—Egypt, Iraq, Yemen, and Morocco—qualify for participation in the MCA based on income. Of these, only Morocco is currently eligible to apply for MCA funds based on its good indicators. (If the income cap is raised in 2006, as has been foreseen, Jordan could also qualify.) The United States must work with other Arab countries to undertake the reforms necessary that would make them eligible for MCA funds. In addition, notwithstanding chronic budget deficits, Washington should devote additional resources for democracy initiatives in the Arab world.

- Arab leaders should understand that a failure to make progress toward democracy will have consequences for their relations with the United States. The United States must convey the message that the general quality of bilateral relations will be contingent, in part, upon reform. In other words, those countries demonstrating democratic progress will benefit from close relations with the United States through expansion of trade relations, military ties, and diplomatic support. Washington should not go so far as to break relations with countries that lag behind, but it should take steps to distance itself from governments that refuse over time to recognize the political rights of their citizens.

In years to come, the world can expect to see both dramatic advances and discouraging reversals in the process of political, economic, and social change in the Middle East. This does not make the Arab world unique. After all, the evolution of American democracy includes not only the majesty of the Declaration of Independence and the Constitution, but also the blight of slavery, a civil war, the denial of women's suffrage for well over a century, and the exclusion of African-Americans from formal participation until the enactment of landmark civil rights legislation in the 1960s. The fits and starts of development in the Middle East are a function of ongoing Arab debates about the appropriate vision for their respective societies. While it is clear that Washington has both compelling interests and a role to play in encouraging change in the Middle East, the emergence of more open polities, greater economic opportunities, and social reform is primarily an Arab project in which Washington can and should play an important supporting role.

Introduction

Across the Arab world, political activists are challenging the status quo. Egyptians are demanding an end to the state of emergency that has been in place almost continuously since the 1950s; Syrians have petitioned their government for political freedoms; Jordanians are seizing new economic opportunities; women in the traditionally conservative Gulf states are seeking wider political and economic participation; even Saudi Arabia is experimenting with elections at the municipal level. In two extraordinary moments in January 2005, the Palestinian and Iraqi people freely elected their leaders. During the following eight weeks, the people of Lebanon forced an end to Syria's military occupation of their country. Political, economic, and social changes are now clearly on the larger Arab agenda.

Against this backdrop, the United States is influencing events in the region through its fight against al-Qaeda, its invasion of Iraq, its demand for reform of Palestinian political institutions, and its call for democracy in the Arab world. The Bush administration's support for political freedom in the Middle East reflects a new reality: In the post–September 11 environment, domestic developments in Arab countries are recognized as a security concern for the United States.

The Independent Task Force on U.S. Policy toward Reform in the Arab World addressed two fundamental questions. First, does a policy of promoting democracy in the Middle East serve U.S. interests and foreign policy goals? Second, if so, how should the United States implement such a policy, taking into account the full range of U.S. interests?

The Task Force's answer to the first question is "yes." Consider the list of challenges facing the Arab world today, from terrorism and regional strife to poverty and violations of human rights; for each, democracy is a necessary component to progress. Adopting a policy that supports democratic reform entails risk in the Middle East. But the dangers of prolonging an unsatisfactory status quo are greater—for people of the region, the United States, and the world. It is also important to underscore that democracy promotion is consistent with American ideals.

The answer to the second question requires consideration of numerous factors, including the absence of a strong democratic tradition within the region, the resistance of Arab leaders to democratic change, America's current credibility problem in the Middle East, and the challenge of moving beyond the relatively simple process of holding elections to the construction of independent and sustainable democratic institutions. Taking each of these factors into account, the Task Force believes that the United States should promote democracy in a manner mindful of the Middle East's political and economic diversity and conscious of the fact that, ultimately, democracy can arise only through Arab efforts. Policymakers should be persistent in support of democratic principles, yet patient in pressing for nonviolent change. America's goal should be to support democratic institutions that are open to participation across the ideological spectrum, excluding only those who refuse to commit to peaceful procedures.

U.S. support for democracy in the Arab world marks a historic change and represents a unique challenge. If the new policy is implemented in ways that are superficial, halfhearted, underfunded, and inconsistent, it will yield new allegations of hypocrisy and further damage relations between the United States and Arab populations. If the United States pushes reform in the region too hard, too fast, this could create instability and undermine U.S. interests. Washington's democracy-promotion policy must be implemented seriously and consistently with respect for democratic principles and a view toward evolutionary, not revolutionary, change. The dangers that accompany rapid change will still be present, but so will the opportunity to create a new and more balanced foundation for Arab stability, and a deeper and stronger basis for friendship between Americans and Arabs. The Task Force has sought to give practical meaning to these guiding principles through the recommendations contained in this report.

Washington's Pro-Democracy Policy

President Bush made democracy in the Middle East a central theme in his second inaugural address and his 2005 State of the Union speech to Congress, arguing that freedom in the United States "depends on the success of liberty in other lands," and calling upon Egypt and Saudi Arabia to take the lead in establishing more open political systems. The president's most widely quoted remarks on the topic took place in November 2003 on the twentieth anniversary of the founding of the National Endowment for Democracy. In that speech, the president laid out the philosophical foundation for his administration's "forward strategy of freedom":

> In many nations of the Middle East—countries of great strategic importance—democracy has not yet taken root. And the question arises: Are the peoples of the Middle East somehow beyond the reach of liberty? I, for one, do not believe it. . . . Champions of democracy in the region understand that democracy is not perfect, it is not the path to utopia, but it is the only path to national success and dignity.

Critics of an American effort to promote and encourage reform in the Middle East argue that change, in particular more open political systems, may place U.S. interests in jeopardy. Analysts argue first that political change and the instability that may result could lead to ethnic conflict or the emergence of Islamist governments opposed to the United States and the West in general. Second, if Washington pushes Arab leaders too hard on reform, contributing to the collapse of friendly Arab governments, this would likely have a deleterious effect on regional stability, peace, and counterterrorism operations. Moreover, there is the risk that too much U.S. pressure for change could result in a backlash against Washington, thereby damaging the credibility of indigenous groups promoting democratic reform. Third, in response to Washington's pressure for political reform, Arab leaders could dig in their heels and actively oppose U.S. policies in the region across the board.

In addition, skeptics of the administration's approach doubt that an emphasis on democracy will do much to weaken the power or attraction of terrorist organizations such as al-Qaeda. The combination of Osama bin Laden's powerful religious imagery and pressing political issues such as the alleged U.S. defilement of Islamic holy lands, the perceived historic injustice perpetrated against the Palestinian people, and a form of globalization that some Arabs believe debases and undermines Arab and Islamic identity indicates that ideology, not democracy, remains paramount for al-Qaeda's theoreticians.

While transitions to democracy can lead to instability in the short term, the Task Force finds that a policy geared toward maintaining the authoritarian status quo in the Middle East poses greater risks to U.S. interests and foreign policy goals. Although political alienation, extremist ideologies, intolerance, and terrorism are, in part, a function of repressive Arab regimes, Washington's support for such regimes has helped make the United States a target of popular discontent. Democracy in the Middle East will not resolve the problem of terrorism, but a more open political environment combined with greater economic opportunity will likely weaken the pull of extremist ideologies that fuel violence. If Arabs are allowed to participate freely and peacefully in the political process, they are less likely to turn to radical measures. If they understand that the United States supports their exercise of liberty, they are less likely to sustain hostile attitudes toward the United States. Efforts to maintain "stability" through the repression of political rights are unlikely to succeed in the long run. The overwhelming empirical evidence clearly indicates that the best kind of stability is democratic stability.

While many Arabs interpret Washington's current rhetorical support for democracy with suspicion, President Bush's public support for change has significant meaning for friends and foes in the region. Some Arab reformers—despite their vehement opposition to the Bush administration's policies regarding Iraq and the Arab-Israeli conflict—indicate that the president's call for democracy has provided them with important political cover to push their own reform agendas. Moreover, the president's support for political change in the Arab world is not limited to his public speeches and large forums. During a White House meeting in February 2004, President Bush emphasized to President

Zine El Abidine Ben Ali, who rules Tunisia with an iron fist, the need for political change. A few months later, in a meeting at his ranch in Crawford, Texas, the president reportedly spoke plainly to Egyptian President Hosni Mubarak about Washington's support for democracy in Egypt.

Despite the administration's new emphasis on democracy in the Middle East, Washington has yet to speak in a consistent way to various Arab countries on the issue. While the Bush administration has often discussed the need for systemic democratic change in the region, it has been inconsistent on specific matters, such as human rights and freedom of expression. The president and his advisers deserve credit for publicly criticizing the Egyptian government's detention of opposition leader Ayman Nour, but they have remained silent on the prison sentences of three Saudi reformers. The administration has also overlooked Bahrain's arrest of bloggers and it has not commented on Jordan's efforts to tamp down on dissent. This sends the wrong signal and damages the credibility of Washington's message about democracy. The United States must take a clear and unwavering stance in support of human rights and freedom of expression throughout the region.

In practice, promoting political, economic, and social change in the Arab world requires a country-by-country approach that recognizes the diversity of opportunities, challenges, and problems that exist in different countries. The tactics the United States employs to promote change in Egypt and Saudi Arabia will not be the same as those used to support reform in Morocco and Yemen. It should also be noted that in some countries, the majority may be content with the status quo. Citizens of Dubai in the United Arab Emirates (UAE), for example, enjoy significant prosperity and stability without democracy. Nevertheless, there are a number of basic principles the United States should emphasize across the region without exception, including human rights, political representation, tolerance, rule of law, women's rights, and transparency of government decision-making.

This report is not about the Arab–Israeli conflict, but the Task Force recognizes that U.S. policy on that subject is relevant to America's standing in the region. Many Arabs see a contradiction between U.S. support for the principles of justice and human rights and its reluctance to criticize Israeli policies toward the Palestinians. The Task Force believes the United States should continue its renewed diplomatic engagement for the purpose of bringing Palestinians and Israelis back to the negotiating table. However, the United States should not accept the argument made by some Arab leaders that progress toward democracy is not possible until the Palestinian question is settled; nor should the United States accept the view espoused by some Israelis that peace negotiations should not resume until the Palestinian Authority is fully democratic. Peace and democracy are mutually reinforcing, but the lack of one should not be used as an excuse for failing to pursue the other. The United States should support democratic reform in the Middle East whether or not there is progress toward peace, as well as support progress toward peace whether or not there is significant democratic reform.

In order to make additional recommendations for U.S. policy, it is necessary to assess and understand the internal political, economic, and social dynamics that have contributed to the myriad difficulties the Middle East currently confronts.

The Arab World:
Politics, Economics, Media,
and Education

Politics and Governance

A Façade of Reform?

Washington's new emphasis on political, economic, and social reform in the Arab world is not occurring in a vacuum. Although the Middle East is often seen as "democracy's desert," there is considerable political dynamism in the Arab world, as activists and reformers have sought to contest the power of their governments. The confluence of internal pressures for change and the emergence of a new generation of young, dynamic leaders such as Jordan's King Abdallah II, Bahrain's King Hamad bin Isa al-Khalifa, the Qatari Emir Sheikh Hamad bin Khalifa al-Thani, and Morocco's King Mohamed VI, as well as U.S. support for reform have, in fact, led to some liberalization.

In December 2002, Bahrain convened its parliament for the first time since 1975. A new constitution, which was ratified in 2002, provides for a variety of individual rights, regularly scheduled elections, and the independence of the judiciary. In April 2004, Algerians reelected President Abdelaziz Bouteflika in balloting that met the European Union's standards, although there were some irregularities in the run-up to the polling. In September of the same year, Qatar promulgated a constitution that gave Qataris new political rights and established a 45-seat Consultative Assembly, two-thirds of which is to be open to direct election. And between January and April 2005, Saudi Arabia held its first nationwide municipal elections. Although a very limited step—women were excluded from the voting—the election can be seen in the context of the royal family's efforts to respond to demands for more political openness. In May 2005, Kuwait's parliament approved the right of women to vote, after years of refusing to do so. Egypt's ruling National Democratic Party (NDP) has embarked on a reform program intended both to modernize the party and to alter Egypt's electoral and political parties' laws, in order to inject a greater measure of pluralism into the political system. And in February 2005, Egyptian President Hosni Mubarak called for an amendment to Article 76 of Egypt's constitution that would permit multiparty presidential elections.

At the same time, however, there is a superficial quality to many of these changes. Often the reforms undertaken do not fundamentally alter the prevailing, nondemocratic rules of the political game. In Qatar, widely considered a regional leader on reform, citizens have expanded political rights, but the 2004 constitution institutionalizes the power of the emir and the al-Thani family. Three Saudis—Ali al-Demaini, Matruq al-Faleh, and Abdullah al-Hamed—were sentenced in May 2005 to prison terms ranging from six to nine years for circulating a petition advocating a constitutional monarchy. Although Bahraini authorities hailed the return of the country's legislature after a twenty-seven-year absence, Bahrain's parliament actually has limited powers. Moreover, Bahraini authorities have arrested human rights activists and bloggers who criticized the government.

In Egypt, the proposed guidelines for amending Article 76 of the constitution are plainly insufficient to enable the opposition to mount an effective challenge to President Mubarak. The government also continues to harass opposition activists. As noted briefly above, the leader of the opposition Hizb al-Ghad (Party of Tomorrow), Ayman Nour, was arrested on what were widely considered trumped-up charges. Nour was ultimately released on bail and is awaiting trial, but the episode may have done significant damage to al-Ghad, undermined Nour's ability to run for president, intimidated other members of Egypt's opposition parties, and further discredited the Egyptian government's claims about reform.

The limited nature of reform in Qatar, Saudi Arabia, Bahrain, and Egypt reflects the continuing problems of governance in the Arab world: the overwhelming power of unelected heads of state, bureaucratic inertia, the lack of rule of law, the absence of a free press, weak political parties, and, of course, the outsized role of security services in politics and society. The justification for this state of affairs has long been national security, notably the perceived Israeli threat and the problem of Islamist extremism. Arab states do have valid security concerns, but these issues have been consistently used to thwart legitimate opposition. Continued arrests and pressure on activists, and reform policies with little substance suggest that Arab leaders are intent on releasing political pressure through some political openings, without pursuing the institutional changes that would alter the authoritarian nature of their political systems.

Although the United States cannot impose democracy on the region, Washington must urge Arab leaders to undertake more than cosmetic changes to their political systems. The Bush administration should encourage Arab leaders to develop public, detailed "pathways to reform" that respond to the specific demands for change by citizens within each Arab country. The public nature of these milestones would help Arab citizens hold their leaders accountable to specific political, economic, and social benchmarks. Such plans should not, however, become empty rhetorical exercises that substitute for real changes in laws and practices. The primary U.S. focus should remain on persuading Arab governments to undertake reforms in response to their citizens' demands.

Islamism and Reform

Across the Middle East, Arab leaders consistently cite the Islamist threat as a prime reason why they cannot risk pursuing political change. They warn that more open political systems will bring to power anti-Western, antidemocratic Islamist groups bent on imposing a theocracy. This warning, in turn, has consistently found a receptive audience in Washington. This is largely a function of Washington's unhappy experience during the Iranian Revolution of 1978–79, which placed U.S. interests in the Persian Gulf in jeopardy. In addition, the aborted Algerian elections of 1991–92 stoked fears within the foreign policy community that political change in the Middle East might foment instability, though it was the military that aborted the elections, setting the stage for Algeria's decade-long plunge into violence.

It is clear that Islamist organizations in the Middle East do not share U.S. goals for the region. At the same time, it is important to distinguish between violent extremist groups (such as al-Qaeda, Islamic Jihad, and the Salafist Group for Preaching and Combat) and other Islamist organizations, including political parties, that have sought to pursue their agenda peacefully (see Appendix A of this report). These nonviolent groups include Egypt's Hizb al-Wasat (Center Party), which has consistently failed to obtain legal recognition; the Islamic Action Front in Jordan; the al-Islah (Reform) Party in Yemen; Bahrain's al-Wefaq (Harmony); Morocco's Justice and Development Party; and Egypt's Muslim Brotherhood, the forebear of many of the Islamist organizations throughout the world. Moreover, it should be recognized that the United Iraqi Alliance—a coalition of Shi'a groups—is one of the leading Islamic democratic movements in the Middle East.

Complicating matters for U.S. policymakers is the existence of hybrid organizations such as Lebanon's Hizballah and Palestine's Islamic Resistance Movement, known by its Arabic acronym Hamas. These organizations are responsible for terrorist attacks that have killed thousands of Israelis, Americans, Europeans, and other Arabs. Hamas-affiliated clerics exhort their followers throughout the West Bank and Gaza Strip to engage in jihad and Hizballah's own satellite television network, al-Manar, preaches hate and incites Arabs across the region against both the United States and Israel. At the same time, however, both groups maintain effective social-service networks that have provided schooling, medical care, and other types of assistance for Palestinians and Lebanese in need. Both have also entered the legitimate political arena. Popularly elected Hizballah representatives have served in Lebanon's parliament since 1992. Although it sat out the Palestinian presidential elections in January 2005, Hamas has significant representation on Palestinian municipal councils and has indicated that it will participate in the Palestinian legislative elections.

Some Arab leaders assert that there is no difference among violent extremist groups, those which have pursued a constitutional strategy, and hybrids like Hamas and Hizballah. In one sense this is demonstrably true: Islamist organizations, by definition, desire the establishment of Islamic states based on shari'a. Some U.S. policymakers and Arab reformers fear that the promotion of democracy could lead to the replacement of one form of authoritarianism with another, i.e., the problem of "one man, one vote, one time." It is important to recognize that there is no incompatibility between being a devout Muslim and a democrat. Yet it is equally important to understand that while Islamist organizations may support democratic procedures as a route to power, they also tend to have a majoritarian view of democracy. This neglects a critical component of democracy: protection of minority rights.

Given the challenges that Islamist groups pose to the United States and its interests in the Middle East, the United States should pursue a four-pronged strategy toward these organizations:

1. Washington must continue to fight Islamist violence and use the full range of foreign policy tools to confront the immediate threat that al-Qaeda and its affiliates pose.

2. While Arab governments have legitimate security concerns, Washington should not accept the use of security as an excuse to justify the suppression of any peaceful political party or organization, including those that are Islamist. Although it is up to Arabs to determine who can participate in their respective political arenas, Washington should make clear to Arab leaders its view that any group willing to abide by the rules and norms of the democratic system—nonviolence, tolerance of opposing views, respect for the rights of all citizens including women and racial and religious minorities, and the rule of law—should be permitted to participate in the political process.

3. Washington should not object to the peaceful political participation of Islamist groups that have been involved in violence in the past, provided they demobilize their military assets and demonstrate a credible commitment to all aspects of the democratic process. Policymakers must recognize, in any case, that

armed organizations such as Hamas and Lebanese Hizballah are already participants in the democratic activities of their societies.

4. To mitigate the possibility that Islamist movements will overwhelm more open Middle Eastern political systems,

    • The United States should support fully competitive elections in parallel with the establishment of the rule of law, judicial independence, changes to electoral laws, and the empowerment of institutions to ensure accountability as well as transparency.

    • Washington should promote constitutional arrangements that would restrain the power of majorities to trample the rights of minorities. Most democracies have mechanisms such as an upper chamber of the legislature chosen on a specialized basis or a supreme court to guard against the "tyranny of the majority." To be sure, these institutions already exist in some Arab countries, but they are often tools that institutionalize the power of the state. Truly independent high courts and safeguards to protect the prerogatives of upper houses of parliaments have the potential to prevent excesses by extremist groups.

In the end, U.S. policymakers must have a realistic sense of what is possible in developing a policy to deal with Islamist groups. Washington currently has little leverage with both violent and nonviolent Islamist groups. Islam plays a central role in Arab societies and Islamism has a powerful appeal throughout the Middle East. As a result, in more open Arab political systems, Islamist movements will likely play an important political role.

Economics

For centuries after the appearance of Islam on the world stage, the Arab world was a global center of learning and progress. Building upon the finest works of ancient classical societies, Arab mathematicians and scientists cast a brilliant light against the gloomy backdrop of medieval Europe. Early Muslims developed the system of numerology still in use today, invented algebra, devised new medical treatments and—

hundreds of years before Christopher Columbus—envisioned a round Earth. Above all, the Arabs were traders, skilled and energetic business-people, looking outward to the opportunities that beckoned from North Africa to South Asia and beyond. The question for the twenty-first century is whether that spirit can be recaptured and renewed.

It is a hopeful sign that most Arab leaders recognize they must address persistent and long-term economic problems, including stagnant growth, un- and underemployment, corruption, and isolation. Indeed, over the last few years, economic development has received the most attention within the councils of Arab governments. There have been signs of economic improvement in Egypt, Jordan, and Morocco, as well as in the Persian Gulf countries, which have embarked on broad plans for regional and global trade integration. For example, Saudi Arabia has undertaken economic reform in order to prepare for World Trade Organization (WTO) membership.

Despite some signs of improvement, Arab economies remain in trouble. Arab leaders want foreign investment and seem willing to undertake reform that attracts this capital, but they also seem reluctant to pursue reforms that would spur the development of liberal market economies. In oil-rich countries, there is still considerable resistance among an elite that enjoys huge oil rents. A fundamental shift to more open, transparent economies would threaten these benefits. In labor-abundant countries there is, of course, concern that economic restructuring will threaten social cohesion as the reduction of subsidies and privatization proceeds. It is encouraging that new economic teams in countries such as Egypt and Jordan have vowed to withstand this type of political pressure, but the potential for backsliding remains considerable. (See Appendix B of this report for recent data on Middle Eastern economies.)

The Arab world's demonstrable lag in the information-technology sector, the increasing imbalance in the Middle East's labor market, and the continued paucity of foreign direct investment in Arab markets underscore the pressing economic problems of Arab countries.

The Middle East and the "Knowledge Economy"

Globalization and the advance of technologies in knowledge-based industries such as telecommunications, information management, and software development provide potential new opportunities for economic growth and development in the Arab world. By all measures, for the Arab world to take advantage of the global "knowledge economy," significant work needs to be done. An examination of how the Middle East fares in comparison to other areas of the world in knowledge-based industries brings into sharp relief just how far the Arab world lags behind. According to the International Telecommunication Union's *World Telecommunication Development Report 2003*, the Middle East ranked above only South Asia and sub-Saharan Africa in Internet users. On average, the number of computers for every 1,000 people was 38, well below the rate in middle- and low-income countries in Europe, Central Asia, Latin America, and the Caribbean. The highest concentration of personal computers in the Arab Middle East was in Saudi Arabia with 130 per 1,000 people. However, in terms of connectivity, the kingdom boasts only twenty-six secure servers. The eighty-three servers in the United Arab Emirates is the largest number of secure servers in the Arab world, but on average, the entire region lags behind all others. In per capita technology spending, the Arab world also trails other regions considerably. Available data indicate that Egypt spent the most in the region on technology per person—roughly $38. By way of comparison, Turkey, which has a slightly smaller population than Egypt and a per capita gross domestic product (GDP) that is a little less than double that of Egypt, spent 3.2 times as much on a per capita basis on technology as did Egypt, while Malaysia, another large developing Muslim country, spent $304 per person (see Appendix C of this report).

There are, of course, bright spots. Egypt is home to two of the region's leading telecommunications firms with business interests across the Middle East. Both companies have won kudos from investors who applaud their management and productivity. In addition, Dubai's "Internet City" has attracted many of the world's leading technology firms. The purpose of that facility, which is built within a free-trade zone, is to provide "a strategic base for companies targeting emerging markets in a vast region extending from the Middle East, the Indian subcontinent, and Africa to the C.I.S. [Commonwealth of Independent States]." It remains unclear how much success the venture will have in fueling economic growth in the region. The leading participants are in business to exploit existing technologies, not to develop new ones. Overall, basic research and development in the Arab world is extremely limited. In 2002, there were 757 patents granted to individuals in Egypt, but only 117 of those individuals were Egyptians. During the same year, Saudi Arabia granted 25 patents, of which only two went to Saudi citizens. In Algeria, only 8 of 111 patents went to resident Algerians. No other countries in the region issued patents. The Republic of Moldova—one of the poorest countries in Europe—granted more patents in 2002 than Saudi Arabia and Algeria combined.

The Arab world's lag in the information- and communications-technology sectors is neither the reason for nor the key to resolving the region's economic woes. Yet the Arab world's deficit in this area is so great that the upside of investment in these areas is likely to produce significant benefits for the region over the long term. As they did with Israel in the late 1980s and the 1990s, the United States and its partners in Europe and Asia should help incubate the development of an Arab technology sector. Specific policies to advance this objective might include a range of financial and non-financial incentives for American and European companies to invest in the region. These might include the creation of investment funds, loan guarantees, and funds for training professionals. While economic incentives for investors can assist technology development, they must coincide with an Arab effort to undertake concrete economic and educational reform. Indeed, one of the most important ways the United States and its allies can promote the development of a scientific infrastructure in the Arab world is through university partnerships and scientific exchanges.

The Labor Market and Foreign Direct Investment

Social dislocation resulting from economic difficulties is cause for significant concern in the Arab world because of imbalances in the Middle Eastern labor market. Although population growth rates in the Middle East are trending down, the region is experiencing a rapid growth in its labor force. Without significant economic growth throughout the Arab world, under- and unemployment will remain a persistent economic and social problem. Previously, public-sector employment and international migration significantly ameliorated these problems. Countries with excess supply of labor such as Egypt, Algeria, Morocco, Syria, and the Palestinian territories could export their workers to the Gulf countries and Europe, where demand for workers was high. These opportunities, however, are rapidly dwindling.

Like North Africa and the Levant, the Gulf countries are facing the challenge of high unemployment and rapid labor-force growth. Some of this unemployment is voluntary, as relatively well-educated members of the middle and upper-middle classes choose to wait for job opportunities in the public sector. Still, not everyone in these countries has this luxury. Members of non-elite classes continue to have difficulty finding quality employment in the private sector. Exacerbating the unemployment problem is the fact that much of the labor force in countries such as Bahrain, Qatar, and Saudi Arabia come from low-wage countries in South and Southeast Asia, pricing both local and imported Arab laborers (Egyptians, Palestinians, and Syrians) out of the market. Many Saudis are squeezed between their own unwillingness to work as laborers and the demands of white-collar employment in the private sector. Both Saudi and foreign companies operating in the kingdom tend to favor expatriate labor for their superior skills.

Europe, another common destination for excess Middle Eastern labor, has begun to close its doors, mostly to North African immigrants. Citing security concerns since 9/11, the Madrid bombings in March 2003, the discovery of extremist cells throughout the continent, as well as rising domestic opposition to Muslim immigration, Europe has begun tightening its southern and eastern borders.

Arab countries need foreign direct investment to ameliorate their excess labor problem. This is a major task given the fact that, outside the energy sector, foreign direct investment is a smaller percentage of GDP in Arab countries than in any other region of the globe. Foreign investors regard the Middle East as a small, fragmented market, rife with cronyism and corruption. China should not be a model for the Arab world, because despite its stunning economic growth, Beijing has yet to undertake significant political reform. Yet, China's experience attracting foreign direct investment holds valuable lessons for Cairo, Rabat, Riyadh, and Amman: specifically, China's disciplined commitment to opening its economy and the clarity and consistency with which it has privatized and liberalized its markets and diversified its economy. Without these changes and concomitant political changes, such as the development and implementation of rules, regulations, and laws that both meet internationally recognized standards and facilitate investment, the international business community will likely continue to view the Middle East as a small and stagnant market.

Washington can use a variety of policy tools, including guarantees and debt financing, to catalyze foreign direct investment in the Middle East. In addition to regional instability, lack of educated workforces, and over-regulation of economies, one of the most important factors hindering investment in the Arab world is the fragmented and small size—in terms of capitalization—of the Middle Eastern market. The limited scope and scale of individual Arab markets are largely unattractive to most investors outside the energy sector.

The Task Force supports the Bush administration's efforts to promote regional economic integration. The Middle East Free Trade Initiative, which the administration unveiled in June 2004, supports WTO membership for Arab countries; expands the generalized system of preferences, which offers goods from six countries of the Middle East and the West Bank and Gaza Strip duty-free entry into the United States; seeks to expand trade through trade and investment framework agreements (TIFAs); promotes investment through bilateral investment treaties; and commits the United States to negotiating bilateral free trade agreements as a stepping-stone to regional economic integration. These are all important initiatives that will provide incentives for Arab leaders to undertake reform and help develop regional economic linkages. Along with these bilateral initiatives, Washington should provide technical assistance to improve regulatory environments, reform tax codes, and most important, remove barriers to intraregional trade in an effort to promote regional economic integration.

The United States should also promote the establishment of QIZs as a stepping-stone to Arab economic integration (see Appendix D of this report). QIZs are areas in which manufactured goods may be exported to the United States under the terms of the U.S.-Israel Free Trade Agreement, provided those goods contain at least 35 percent local content and 11.7 percent Israeli content. Since the establishment of thirteen QIZs in Jordan in 1999, the volume of Jordanian-Israeli trade and Jordanian exports to the United States has increased exponentially. A caveat is in order: QIZs are promising tools to promote economic development, but only if there is a critical mass of them. Limited numbers of QIZs can negatively affect economic competition and further skew the distribution of wealth in countries where they exist. The United States should promote the development of as many as one hundred or more QIZs in the Middle East. This would foster greater competition, improve efficiency, and ultimately deliver lower-cost, higher-quality goods to consumers both in the Arab world and in the United States.

Corruption, which is a major problem throughout the developing world, remains an obstacle to foreign direct investment in the Middle East, where there is limited competition and excessive government control. One of the surest ways to reduce corruption is through deregulation and greater integration with the international business community. With less regulation there are usually fewer opportunities for bureaucrats and others close to the state to demand kickbacks, payoffs, or commissions. Greater integration with global businesses will allow both companies and entrepreneurs to access capital based on what they do, not who they know.

Another essential instrument in the fight to control corruption is the establishment of truly independent and resourceful counter-corruption commissions. Algeria's Audit Office and Egypt's Central Auditing Organization have the structures in place to carry out these functions, but they need to be empowered. The United States should provide assistance that would either further develop the capacity of these organizations to conduct investigations or help establish them where they do not exist.

Economic development in the Middle East makes good commercial sense for the Arab world, the United States, Europe, and Asia. The multilateral effort by the Group of Eight (G8) to spur investment in the Middle East is a good start to addressing some of the fundamental economic difficulties Arabs confront. In addition, one of the best ways the United States and its partners can spur economic development in parts of the Arab world is to secure an agreement in the Doha Round on agriculture. The opening of European agricultural markets would substantially benefit countries such as Morocco and Tunisia.

A final note on the interconnectedness between economics and politics is necessary. First, it is important to recognize that the institutions of Middle Eastern economies are critical components of the very foundations of the authoritarian systems of the region. Arab leaders are reluctant to undertake reform because economic change will likely undermine support for their regimes. Second, Washington has tended to promote economic reform and growth in the hope that political change will inevitably result from economic reform. Although intrinsically important, all the available social science data indicate that economic growth is crucial for the durability of democracies but does not directly cause democracy. Finally, favoring policies to promote economic reform at the expense of political reform ignores the real political demands of Arab citizens. For all these reasons, debates about sequencing economic change before political reform are misplaced. Rather, economic and political reform must be undertaken simultaneously.

Media

An additional indication that the Arab world is undergoing a transition is the emergence of what have come to be known as the "new Arab media." Where media were once the exclusive province of bureaucratic and moribund ministries of information, there has been a significant democratization of information in the Middle East since the late 1990s. Arabs have increased access to alternative information through the Internet, satellite television, and new print media.

Satellite Television

In 1996, the Arab satellite news channel al-Jazeera was launched and it has had a powerful effect on local politics. The subject of countless news articles, reports, and commentaries, the network has confounded Arab leaders and American officials, to the delight of al-Jazeera's large and growing audience. The Doha-based network was not, in fact, the first Arab satellite news channel. Saudi-owned Middle East Broadcasting Center (MBC), which is a news and entertainment channel, began broadcasting from London in 1991, though the network is now head-quartered in Dubai's "Media City." Although MBC was the first Arab satellite network, al-Jazeera truly revolutionized the format and content of Arab news networks.

Along with its news programs, al-Jazeera appropriated the talk show format. Programs such as *Crossfire, The O'Reilly Factor*, and *Hardball*, which have become influential in shaping public opinion in the United States, now have functional equivalents in al-Jazeera's programming line-up. It is these programs—*Akthar min Ra'y* (Multiple Views), *Bila Hudud* (Without Limits), and *Ittijah al-Muakis* (Opposite Direction)—that have proved to be both path-breaking and controversial. Through-out the region, opponents of Arab regimes across the political spectrum, Israelis, Americans, and Europeans have had an opportunity to offer their views on this channel. Much of this debate angered Arab officialdom, resulting in efforts to ban al-Jazeera or close its offices in a variety of countries.

The success of al-Jazeera has spawned copycats, including its closest competitor, al-Arabiyya, which MBC owns and also broadcasts from Dubai. Others include Abu Dhabi Television, and the notorious al-Manar, a propaganda organ for Lebanese Hizballah. (See Appendix E of this report for a listing of major Arab satellite television networks.) In addition, Arab satellite television has forced state-run media outlets in the region to compete for viewers, necessitating changes in both the style and the content of broadcasts.

The Bush administration has been vocal in its criticism of Arab satellite channels, but particularly of al-Jazeera. During the U.S. military campaigns in Afghanistan and Iraq, the administration accused al-Jazeera's producers and reporters of purposely stoking anti-Americanism with reporting based more on rumor and innuendo than on solid journalism. The network's correspondents respond that they are only telling the Afghan and Iraqi stories that Western, particularly U.S., audiences do not see due to the bias of America's own media outlets. Yet, at the same time, al-Jazeera, al-Arabiyya, and the other networks are also responding to a more competitive Arab media environment.

In time, the Arab satellite news industry will likely develop a variety of tiers, from the decidedly lowbrow to more sophisticated program-ming. Al-Arabiyya's recent effort to move away from some of the shock-value type reporting and commentary that has become al-Jazeera's stock-in-trade may be an early indication that Arab satellite news networks are starting to diversify along these lines.

While it is appropriate for Americans and U.S. policymakers to criticize what they regard as inaccurate and biased coverage on Arab satellite news networks, it is counterproductive for the U.S. government to exert pressure on Arab governments to alter the content broadcast on these stations. To be sure, there are problems with the Arab media as there are in other parts of the world, but the credibility of Washington's message about freedom of expression, individual rights, and tolerance is damaged as a result of heavy-handed efforts to censor material broadcast to Arab homes. Instead, U.S. officials, preferably those with Arabic language skills, should more actively engage the Arab media in an effort to explain Washington's policy in the region.

The Internet and Print Media

Although the Middle East lags behind other regions in connectivity, those Arabs who are connected to the Internet have ready access to the information revolution. Although some Arab countries, notably Saudi Arabia, Syria, and Tunisia, either censor what websites can be seen in their countries or monitor what people are looking at on the Web, the Internet has become a valuable tool for Arabs to reach beyond the borders of the state-controlled press. Web logs (also known as "blogs") are gaining popularity in the Arab world for their unvarnished commentary on important issues of the day. For example, Bahrainis dissatisfied with the way the traditional press covered the 2002 scandal involving the national pension fund, GOSI, could visit the "Bahraini blogsite" or "Mahmood's Den" on the Internet for a more trenchant analysis of that episode.

When one thinks of "new media," newspapers and magazines do not readily come to mind. Yet there are also changes underway in this area. New newspapers and magazines have cropped up throughout the region. Their editors are determined to engage in debates previously off-limits. In Egypt, the English-language weekly *Cairo Times* set a standard for outspoken criticism of the Egyptian government. In mid-2004, *al-Masri al-Yom* was launched and immediately ignored unwritten codes in Egypt's Arabic press about criticizing President Mubarak and members of his family. Jordan's privately owned Arabic daily, *al-Ghad*, has established a reputation for quality. Well-established newspapers, such as Saudi Arabia's *al-Watan* and the Saudi-owned, London-produced *al-Hayat*, have published articles openly questioning a variety of previously taboo subjects including the role of women in society, extremism, and the intersection of religion and politics.

These developments are important and indicate a significant opening in Arab societies. And while Arab governments do not necessarily like the debates that are taking place around them, the trend toward more open discussion of critical issues confronting Arab societies is unlikely to be reversed. Arab satellite news channels, Arabic-content websites, and the increasingly bold print media have become popular.

The emergence of the new Arab media is a positive development. There are two specific areas where the United States can encourage further development of new and independent Arab media. First, Washington should provide technical assistance to establish the regulatory framework for private media markets. To be sure, Arab governments are reluctant to give up their monopoly over the airwaves and control—direct or indirect—of the media. Still, the United States should not shy away from promoting this important change. A more democratic environment will provide Arab media consumers with more choice and better quality. Second, concomitant with Washington's push for privatization of Arab media should be an emphasis on improving laws that protect freedom of speech.

Washington should also work with American media companies and universities to establish exchange programs aimed at enhancing the professionalism of Arab journalists. The Fulbright fellowship program should be extended or a new fellowship program created to include Arab journalists. In addition, American journalists must develop a greater expertise on the Middle East and broaden their contacts to include reformers and opposition activists.

The United States should also leverage the new media space in the region to spread its message about democracy and freedom. On balance, the United States has done a poor job in this area. Although Radio Sawa, which the Broadcasting Board of Governors established in March

2002, is a relative success among younger Arabs, with its mix of American and Arabic pop music and regular news bulletins, it is unclear what affect the station is having on the way Arabs view the United States. The Arabic Service of the Voice of America was defunded in favor of Radio Sawa. This was a mistake, as VOA's Arabic service and Radio Sawa serve different functions and audiences. Whereas Radio Sawa is geared exclusively toward Arab youth, the VOA has traditionally provided news and information from and about the United States for a wider-range audience, including elites. The service should become an integral component of Washington's public diplomacy strategy, emphasizing reform issues in addition to news and information about the United States.

Washington should also rethink the role of its own Arabic satellite channel, al-Hurra. Because the channel is operated by the U.S. government, the suspicion is strong within the region that it is merely a conveyor of propaganda. This critique will continue to hamper al-Hurra's efforts to draw a larger market share, especially in comparison to al-Jazeera and al-Arabiyya. There is, however, an important programming niche that al-Hurra could fill, which has the advantage of being pro-reform without the taint of the U.S. government. Some of al-Hurra's programming should be shifted to a C-SPAN-style format. Broadcasting the processes of the U.S. and other democratic governments, including congressional and parliamentary hearings, political rallies, and debates, would expose Arabs to the spectacle of free political systems in action.

Education

Since the September 11 attacks on New York and Washington, there has been much media attention on education reform in the Middle East, based on the assumption that Arab education systems are producing young graduates particularly prone to extremist recruitment. Whether or not this is true, there has been a growing awareness in the Arab world since the mid-1990s that Arab education systems are not producing students equipped with the skills necessary for a global economy.

Yet the problems of Arab education systems are more profound than merely preparing students better in math and science. At a narrow level, the challenges confronting Arab education systems include chronic underfunding, oversized classes, minimally proficient instructors, disconnected parents, emphasis on testing and rote memorization, as well as ideological battles over curricula. More broadly, Arab educational systems reflect the bigger problem of politics and governance in the Middle East: an overweening, paternalistic, minimally legitimate state. Arab education systems have become instruments of political control.

Still, Arab countries have made some modest progress in educational reform. For example, although there are big gaps in primary education in countries such as Egypt, Morocco, and Yemen, access to all levels of education for women has increased. In fact, at Arab universities, female enrollment almost equals male enrollment. The exceptions are Bahrain, the United Arab Emirates, Saudi Arabia, Qatar, and Oman, where women outnumber men at the universities. At all levels of education, there is an ongoing internal reevaluation of textbooks—perhaps most significant in Saudi Arabia. The increase in adult literacy throughout the Middle East is faster than anywhere else in the world. While impressive, it is important to note that the Arab world has a long way to go in this area, as only two-thirds of Egyptians and only half of Moroccans and Yemenis are literate. In addition, there has been an increase in English-language instruction, and in most engineering, general sciences, and medical faculties, English is the language of instruction. Finally, Arab educators have begun to explore an accreditation system for Arab colleges and universities.

The Qataris have undertaken two innovative steps to correct what they clearly perceive to be deficits in their own educational system. The Qatar Foundation built "Education City"—a complex composed of leading American universities such as Georgetown, Carnegie Mellon, Weill Cornell Medical College, Virginia Commonwealth School of Arts, and Texas A&M—which will train Arab doctors, scientists, and engineers. Education City has begun by serving elites, but the Qatar Foundation has also invited the Rand Corporation to develop charter schools, revamp the public K–12 education system, and implement reforms at Qatar University. Education City and the Rand project are excellent examples of what U.S. educational organizations and the private sector can do to further educational development in the region.

It is important to account for the question of religion and education. It is only since September 11 that the word *madrasah* has taken on sinister connotations in the West. Indeed, before they became associated with extremism and violence, the *madaaris* (plural of *madrasah*) system of religious education played an important role, primarily in South Asia, picking up the slack where public education systems had failed. To be sure, these schools maintained a significant religious component to their curricula, but only a small number can fairly be called breeding grounds for terrorists. In fact, none of the nineteen hijackers on September 11 were products of this system, though surely many followers of Osama bin Laden are. That being said, it is important for U.S. officials to recognize that religion is and will likely remain an important component of the curricula in many Arab countries.

Official U.S. involvement in educational reform is fraught with political, diplomatic, and cultural pitfalls and must be approached with care and sensitivity. The Task Force supports the Bush administration's approach to this issue, which treats education reform primarily as an economic priority rather than a social or cultural problem.

Education reform is an area where the United States should seek the partnership of American, European, and Asian educational institutions, foundations, the private sector, and multilateral organizations. Specifically, Washington should develop teacher-training programs based both in the United States and the Middle East, provide technical assistance to decentralize Arab educational systems, help further expand English-language instruction in the region, and help establish lifelong learning through adult education programs.

In addition, given Washington's goal of promoting economic and scientific development in the Middle East, Washington should also promote partnerships between U.S. business and engineering schools and Arab educational institutions. While U.S.-style education in the Arab world (such as establishing a program in Qatar's Education City) is an important measure, Washington should continue to foster exchanges to bring Arab students to the United States.

While recognizing the delicate balance the Department of Homeland Security must strike between protecting the country and maintaining its traditional openness to foreign students, Washington must streamline its visa policies to allow students from the Arab world to enter the United States. If the visa process continues to prevent or deter Arabs from visiting the United States, Washington will be cutting off a wide range of worthy cultural, educational, and scientific exchanges.

Teacher training and professional education are critically important to the future of the region. At the same time, there is a paucity of Arabic translations of the world's "great books." Washington should provide grants through organizations like the National Endowment for Democracy to translate these works. This would help expose Arab students to a greater variety of thought from around the world.

Current U.S. Approaches to Promoting Democracy: How Effective?

Since September 11, the United States has pursued several different approaches to forging change in the Middle East. The first is warfare. Although the suspicion that Saddam Hussein possessed weapons of mass destruction and his alleged ties to al-Qaeda were the primary, though ultimately unfounded, reasons for Operation Iraqi Freedom, the Bush administration also regarded the totalitarian nature of Saddam's regime as moral justification for the invasion. Prior to the war, the president stated his conviction that a stable and democratic Iraq could serve as a model for the entire Arab world.

The situation in Iraq remains uncertain as the insurgency continues and the political situation evolves. The invasion has not helped America's standing or credibility in the region, nor do many Arabs look at Iraq and say, "I wish my country could be like that." At the same time, there is evidence that the removal of Saddam Hussein and the first round of elections (in January 2005) have contributed to the momentum for change. Arab political activists may vehemently disagree with U.S. policy but still find value in the example of Iraqis forming political parties, electing leaders, and drafting a new constitution.

Beyond President Bush's use of military force, his administration has sought to support reform through two primary regionwide initiatives. The Middle East Partnership Initiative was established in 2002 with the express purpose of coordinating and managing the U.S. government's reform agenda in the areas of economics, politics, education, and women's issues. In practice, MEPI has sought to encourage trade, mobilize foreign direct investment, promote the rule of law, strengthen civil society, help improve access to and quality of education, and address challenges that women face in the Arab world. Some of this work was begun during the 1990s under the auspices of the U.S. Agency for International Development (USAID), but the exigencies of post–September 11 U.S. foreign policy have given many of these programs new emphasis. Moreover, while USAID's work has focused to some extent on creating constituencies within Arab governments for change, the rationale for MEPI was to work with independent and indigenous NGOs and civil-society groups, as well as with governments.

After initial funding of $29 million in 2002, MEPI received a sharp increase in funding for fiscal year (FY) 2003. This level of funding was not carried over the following year, however. The administration requested $145 million for FY 2004, but Congress appropriated only $45 million for the effort. The table in Appendix F of this report makes clear that the bulk of USAID funding in FY 2003 and FY 2004 was devoted to the construction of new political institutions in Iraq.

Despite its intended emphasis on building Arab civil society, a majority of MEPI's first $100 million was spent on programs that target Arab government agencies and employees, including bureaucrats, teachers, parliamentarians, and judges. The relative differences in spending among different programs are not necessarily indicative that Washington is more interested in one area than in others. For example, it would be incorrect to assert that the significant disparity between funding for women's issues and the other pillars suggests Washington's lack of interest in this critically important area. Rather, it is important to recognize that programs designed to assist Arab governments to undertake, for example, education reform are more expensive than those dedicated to improving the status of women. In addition, it is important to understand that there are obstacles to funding small NGOs. Since September 11, the United States has implemented an exhaustive review process and instituted strict requirements to safeguard against funding organizations that might support terror. The problems are not all with

U.S. government regulations, however. Historically, the Egyptian government confined USAID's work to issue areas and groups Cairo deemed appropriate, at times hindering U.S. efforts. This has changed recently with the passage of the Brownback Amendment to the omnibus appropriations bill for the State Department and foreign operations. The Brownback Amendment allows USAID to direct the use of U.S. funds for democracy programs in Egypt in coordination with an independent board of prominent Egyptian political activists and experts.

The Brownback Amendment underlines the importance of Congress's role in promoting democracy in the Middle East. Given that Congress controls the purse strings of the U.S. government, it must fulfill its oversight responsibilities regarding how taxpayer money is being spent in the Arab world. Members of Congress have also been active sponsoring a variety of accountability acts, which would impose sanctions on a variety of countries, including Saudi Arabia and Egypt, to force Arab leaders to modify their policies and ultimately undertake political reform. While sanctions may be appropriate for Syria and formerly for Saddam Hussein's Iraq, punitive congressional measures against U.S. allies can damage relations, making it more difficult for Washington to achieve its objectives and further contributing to anti-Americanism in the region.

The *Partnership for Progress for a Common Future with the Region of the Broader Middle East and North Africa* (commonly referred to as the Broader Middle East Initiative) emerged from the June 2004 G8 summit. This initiative, the U.S. government's overarching multilateral frame of reference for promoting reform in the Middle East, has four primary components. The first, the "Forum for the Future," is modeled on the Asia-Pacific Economic Cooperation forum (APEC) and is designed to foster communication on reform-related issues. It includes government-to-government talks intended to offer political support and technical advice to Middle Eastern leaders interested in undertaking reform. There are also sessions to bring together civil society activists and business leaders to talk about reform with Arab leaders. Second, the partnership also emphasizes economic development via microfinance programs; enhanced support for small and medium-sized businesses, entrepreneurship, and training to expand job growth; and, finally, programs intended to expand regional investment. Third, the G8 has committed support for a regionwide literacy program intended to halve illiteracy rates by 2015. Finally, the Partnership for Progress established the "Democracy Assistance Dialogue" that would bring together development institutions in the Middle East, foundations, and international financial institutions—such as the World Bank and the International Monetary Fund (IMF)—to coordinate the use of resources to support political and economic change.

MEPI, which principally supports the political goals of the Partnership for Progress, and the partnership itself represent important tools to promote change in the Middle East. Both initiatives faithfully reflect the Bush administration's belief that the nature of governance and politics in Arab countries has a direct effect on the national security of the United States. Yet, as important as MEPI and the Partnership for Progress are, the Task Force detects a number of problems with them.

First, Washington's European partners remain skeptical of efforts to promote democracy in the Middle East. European reluctance undermines the potential efficacy of pursuing reform through an initiative like the Partnership for Progress. The tortured process of establishing the initiative (over both Arab and European objections) holds out the prospect that the partnership's already rather tame set of programs will be further diluted over time. Despite these problems, Washington should remain engaged with its European allies to promote change in the Middle East. There should be an annual G8 review of the partnership's activities and progress. Some specific areas in which the United States and Europe can collaborate include providing assistance for education reform, frameworks for the development of a private media market, and importantly, human rights. Although the European record on defending Muslim lives is less than stellar (as evidenced in Bosnia and Darfur), the human rights abuses at Abu Ghraib in Iraq and revelations of inhumane treatment of Muslim prisoners at Camp X-Ray in Guantanamo Bay damage Washington's credibility on this issue. Despite a history of European colonial domination, the perception of Europe in the Arab world is better than that of the United States. Consequently, it may be helpful for the European Union to take the lead promoting human rights in the Arab world.

Second, the Bush administration deserves credit for devoting more resources than ever before to economic development, women's issues, education, and civil society—the core components of MEPI. The Task Force believes these programs are vitally important to helping individuals in the Arab world and should be continued, but they are focused almost exclusively on building grassroots demand for democracy. As recent events in Iraq, the Palestinian territories, Lebanon, and Egypt suggest, there is ample demand for democracy and freedom. Moreover, civil society, economic development, women's rights, and education all have net social welfare benefits, but they are not sufficient to cause democratic change. The problem is actually with the supply side of the democracy equation, i.e., the durability of the authoritarian state and the profound reluctance of many Arab leaders to open their political systems. Consequently, the U.S. government's most important tool to promote democracy is direct engagement with Arab governments, most of which must be done behind the scenes.

In order to support voices for political, economic, and social change in the Middle East more effectively, the Task Force believes that the policy component of MEPI should remain within the State Department, but the bulk of MEPI's funds should be shifted to an outside independent organization such as the National Endowment for Democracy, AMIDEAST, or a newly created Middle East foundation. Many Middle Eastern NGOs are reluctant to accept direct transfers from an arm of the U.S. government, fearing that this would taint these organizations in the eyes of their constituencies.

More broadly, the United States should also carefully consider the way in which it provides aid to Arab allies. Although there may be instances when threats to cut aid or the application of sanctions are appropriate, these policies also run the risk of precipitating a backlash against the United States, potentially undermining Washington's ability to encourage political, economic, and social change. Rather than cutting aid, the Bush administration should think carefully about how aid resources are spent and the political implications of current aid programs. For example, rather than focusing on military-to-military relations in narrowly defined, technical areas, Washington can use its support for militaries across the region to promote democratic reform within these important organizations. The United States should increase its International Military Education and Training program (IMET) to accomplish this goal. Currently only nine Arab militaries participate in IMET, which brings officers to the United States for training. Courses are designed to increase the technical proficiency of Arab armies, but also include topics such as rule of law, democratic values, and recognized standards of human rights.

The United States currently provides approximately $5.5 billion annually in economic and military assistance to the Arab world, excluding reconstruction assistance for Iraq. As a general principle, the United States should use the promise of additional financial support as an incentive for reform. Although it has yet to dispense aid, the United States already has a program that would condition aid in this way to poor countries—mostly in Africa and Asia—called the Millennium Challenge Account. The funds will be distributed to those countries that have per capita income below a certain level (in 2005, below $1,465) and are best able to use them based on sixteen specific reform-related criteria including accountability, rule of law, education reform, and economic freedom. Currently, only four Arab countries—Egypt, Iraq, Yemen, and Morocco—qualify for participation in the MCA based on income. Of these only Morocco is currently eligible to apply for MCA funds based on its good indicators. (If the income cap is raised in 2006, as has been foreseen, Jordan could also qualify.) The United States must work with other Arab countries to undertake the reforms necessary to make them eligible for MCA funds. In addition, notwithstanding chronic budget deficits, Washington should devote additional resources for democracy initiatives in the Arab world. The potential return from supporting more democratic political systems in the Middle East is well worth the price.

The United States wields considerably less leverage when it comes to wealthy countries of the Gulf such as Saudi Arabia, Qatar, Bahrain, and the United Arab Emirates, none of which needs Washington's financial assistance. Recognizing this limitation, the Bush administration can still promote change effectively by widening its circle of contacts in the Gulf to include reformers, pressing the issue of election monitors, and continuing to use the presidential bully pulpit to praise those countries that have undertaken reform and single out those that have lagged behind.

Arab leaders should understand that a failure to make progress toward democracy will have consequences for their relations with the United States. The United States must convey the message that the general quality of bilateral relations will be contingent, in part, upon reform. In other words, those countries demonstrating democratic progress will benefit from close relations with the United States through expansion of trade relations, military ties, and diplomatic support. Washington should not go so far as to break relations with countries that lag behind, but it should take steps to distance itself from governments that refuse over time to recognize the political rights of their citizens.

Conclusion

The United States's long history of working with nondemocratic leaders in the Middle East has damaged U.S. credibility in the region. Although a policy predicated on political, economic, and social change in the Arab world may present some short-term risks to Washington's interests, these risks are worth taking. The long-run benefits of a more democratic and economically developed Middle East outweigh the potential challenges Washington might confront in the foreseeable future.

More open Middle Eastern polities and economies will likely have four positive interrelated effects. First, although extremism will certainly continue to exist in the region, forces of moderation and tolerance will have greater opportunity to frame the terms of debate in a more open political environment. Second, political, economic, and social reform will likely, over time, reduce the reservoir of recruits to extremist organizations such as al-Qaeda and others that target the United States and Americans. In addition, there is substantial evidence to support the "democratic peace theory," which posits that democracies do not fight each other. Although it is true that countries in transition may be more belligerent, the emergence of democracy in the Middle East would, over the long run, reduce the likelihood of interstate conflict in the region.

Finally, although there is no guarantee, in the long run U.S. support for change in the region will also likely improve Washington's relations with the Arab world. Recent public-opinion polls show that, in addition to Washington's support for Israel, the seemingly significant gap between the principles that ostensibly guide U.S. conduct in the world—freedom, liberty, and self-determination—and objective reality produces outrage in the Arab world. To be sure, the quality of governance in the Arab world is an Arab responsibility, but many in the region simply cannot understand why a country whose democratic institutions they so admire provides political, economic, and military aid to absolute monarchs and military dictators. The United States should continue to promote and offer both political and financial support for political change, economic restructuring, and social reform.

There will be both dramatic advances and discouraging reversals in the process of political, economic, and social change in the Middle East. This does not make the Arab world unique. After all, the evolution of American democracy includes not only the majesty of the Declaration of Independence and the Constitution, but also the blight of slavery, a civil war, denial of women's suffrage for well over a century, and the exclusion of African-Americans from full participation until the enactment of landmark civil rights legislation in the 1960s. The fits and starts of development in the Middle East are a function of ongoing Arab debates about the appropriate vision for their respective societies. While it is clear that Washington has both compelling interests and a role to play in encouraging change in the Middle East, the emergence of more open polities, greater economic opportunities, and social reform is primarily an Arab project in which Washington can and must play an important supporting role.

Additional or Dissenting Views

I endorse the findings of this report with one exception. Regarding how to ensure that extremists do not come to dominate democratic systems, the report suggests that upper houses of parliament selected on a specialized basis could be part of the answer. This might be interpreted as endorsing unelected upper houses as permanent fixtures in Arab countries. The United States should promote the establishment of checks and balances within fully democratic systems, which might include such instruments as detailed rules of the political game and bills of citizens' rights to which all participants must agree, as well as judiciaries empowered to enforce the rules.

Michele D. Dunne

The report does not adequately address the risks to American interests posed by possible electoral victories by Islamist parties and groups in the Arab world. Even the most moderate and nonviolent of Arab Islamist parties disagree with American goals on Arab-Israeli issues and would not be willing to accept the kind of influence the United States now exercises in the region. As Islamists are the major opposition group in every Arab state—Lebanon is a complicated exception—with access to organizational resources denied to other political tendencies, they will undoubtedly benefit disproportionately from moves toward electoral politics. The report urges a dual track of social-economic-educational reform contemporaneous with moves toward freer electoral politics. I believe that American policy should be concentrated on encouraging an evening of the playing field for non-Islamist political tendencies in the Arab world, supporting more liberal movements and individuals, before real elections. Our policy should be self-consciously and openly biased toward those groups in Arab society which are more accepting of our foreign policy views and come closer to our own political values. That will mean confronting Arab regimes more often and more openly in support of such groups, but will also mean dropping the focus on elections adopted by the Bush administration.

The report also uncritically accepts the assertion that terrorism goes down as democracy increases. I find neither empirical nor theoretical support for this assertion. Support for democratic reform may serve a number of purposes, but it is unlikely to effect the level of anti-American terrorism emanating from the Arab world.

F. Gregory Gause III

Enthusiastically signing our report, I offer from my perspective five pointed verities to advance Arab democracy.

Arab democracy has to be culturally Islamic. As federalist American democracy bears the cast of Enlightenment deism, Islam can and shall powerfully undergird Arab democracy. There is no inconsistency in this assertion. American democratization efforts must embrace that reality.

Arab economic advance predetermines Arab political advance. Our report ascribes basically the same relative importance to political progress and economic progress. Here I dissent, but only slightly. Economics is demonstrably the independent variable—the factor over which the United States has an immense measure of international influence. Politics is the dependent variable—the result affects where the world will observe democratic outcomes of a vigorous global free-market economy with much more significant Arab-nation participation. Arabs understand economic subtleties and the influence of commerce on democracy far better than Washington, the European Union, or the western academy credits them.

The U.S.-Israel relationship permeates Arab democratic discourse. Arabs in all social classes and at every level of educational achievement believe that Washington's support of Israel is automatic, reflexive, and entirely uncritical. This view, often quite nuanced, persistently impedes the advance of Arab democracy. The extent to which the United States directly addresses this view as a basic misperception will enhance our democratizing influence in the region and among Arabs worldwide.

"Democracy and reforms cannot be imposed from outside" (quote from Saudi Crown Prince Abdullah in *Le Monde*, April 13, 2005). The Abdullah formulation is precisely correct and it really is the bedrock of our report. Washington can help by nurturing the global environment for evolutionary democratization and accelerating progressive change through economic enhancement and public diplomacy.

Abu Ghraib matters infinitely more than Americans realize. Its effects are enduring. These human rights abuses were a stunning desecration of American values and a psychological assault on Islam. No one with whom I conduct business in Arab nations has "moved on," even in this remarkable "Arab Spring."

Michael N. Pocalyko

While we agree with the overall thrust of this report, and believe that the time for democracy and reform has come to the Arab world, we would like to stress three points that deserve more emphasis.

The shape of Arab democracy and reform will be what the Arabs themselves make of it. To be sustainable, Arab democracy must have an Arab and an Islamic character, and be built from within the society. Democracy and reform will succeed only when Arab officials and religious and private-sector leaders address self-defeating behavior such as demagogy and religious fanaticism. Yet reform deserves support from the United States, as well as from Europe and others, including, for example, India. For this effort to be successful, Arab leaders and reformers must work together.

The Arab economic situation is not as dire as the report implies. Arabs do not lack capital, although an estimated $1.3 trillion of Arab capital is outside the region and needs to be brought back. Bringing it back would require domestic stability and a business-friendly policy. For example, Arab market capitalization at the end of 2004 was valued at $900 billion, compared to the figure for East Asia (including China but excluding Japan) of $1.2 trillion. But democratization and reform can help reinvigorate these economies. Economic progress in the Gulf is impressive but more resources need to go into modern education, including science, technology, and business.

The importance of the Arab-Israeli conflict to democracy and reform should not be minimized. Over more than five decades, the conflict has caused enormous suffering and economic malaise for both Arabs and Israelis and has bolstered authoritarian rule and extremism. Its continuation hampers reform and, in order to support democracy, a major effort must be made to resolve it, and this requires the personal engagement of the American president. Peace can only enhance democracy and economic prosperity.

William A. Rugh
and
Odeh F. Aburdene

Task Force Members

Feisal Abdul Rauf is the Founder and Chairman of the American Society for Muslim Advancement (ASMA) and of the Cordoba Initiative, a multifaith organization whose objective is to heal the relationship between the Islamic world and the United States by 2015. He is also the Imam of Masjid al-Farah, a mosque in New York City. He is a member of the World Economic Forum's Council of 100 Leaders and a Trustee of the Islamic Cultural Center of New York. His writing includes *Islam: A Search for Meaning* and *Islam: A Sacred Law*. His latest book, *What's Right with Islam: A New Vision for Muslims and the West*, ranked among the *Christian Science Monitor's* five best nonfiction books of 2004.

Khaled M. Abou El Fadl is Professor of Law at the University of California, Los Angeles, and a prominent scholar in Islamic law. He serves on the board of Human Rights Watch and as a Commissioner on the United States Commission on International Religious Freedom. He was previously a Visiting Professor at Yale Law School.

Odeh F. Aburdene* is President of OAI Advisors, an advisory firm providing investment, economic, business, and energy expertise on the Middle East. He is also an adviser to Capital Partners Holding. Previously, Dr. Aburdene served as Vice President for Middle East Business at Occidental Petroleum and First National Bank of Chicago. He sits

---

* The individual has endorsed the report and submitted an additional or a dissenting view.
Note: Task Force members participate in their individual and not institutional capacities.

49

on the Board of AMIDEAST, Search for Common Ground, the Rand Center for Middle East Public Policy, the Bethlehem Foundation, and Seeds of Peace. He also serves on the Advisory Board of the Fletcher School of Law and Diplomacy.

Madeleine K. Albright is Co-Chair of the Task Force and Principal of the Albright Group LLC. She is also Chairman of the National Democratic Institute and serves on the Board of the New York Stock Exchange. Dr. Albright served as Secretary of State under President Bill Clinton.

Nancy Birdsall is the founding President of the Center for Global Development. Prior to launching the center, she served for three years as Senior Associate and Director of the Economic Reform Project at the Carnegie Endowment for International Peace. From 1993 to 1998, she was Executive Vice President of the Inter-American Development Bank. Before joining the Inter-American Development Bank, she spent fourteen years in research, policy, and management positions at the World Bank. She is the author, co-author, or editor of more than a dozen books, academic articles, and monographs including, most recently, *Financing Development: The Power of Regionalism* and *Delivering on Debt Relief: From IMF Gold to a New Aid Architecture.*

Daniel M. Brumberg is Special Adviser for the Muslim World Initiative at the United States Institute of Peace, where he focuses on issues of democratization and political reform in the Middle East and the wider Islamic world. He is also an Associate Professor at Georgetown University and a former Senior Associate in the Democracy and Rule of Law Project at the Carnegie Endowment for International Peace. He is Chairman of the Foundation on Democratization and Political Change in the Middle East, a member of the Advisory Board of the International Forum on Democratic Studies, and a member of the Editorial Boards of the *Journal of Democracy* and *Political Science and Politics.*

Leslie Campbell is Director of the Middle East and North Africa Programs of the National Democratic Institute for International Affairs. He is a member of the Board of Directors of the Institute for Media, Policy and Civil Society (IMPACS), and a Fellow at the Queen's

University Center for the Study of Democracy. Before his position at the National Democratic Institute, Mr. Campbell served as Chief of Staff to the leader of the New Democratic Party in the Canadian House of Commons.

Steven A. Cook is Project Director of the Task Force and a Next Generation Fellow at the Council on Foreign Relations, where he specializes in Arab politics and U.S. Middle East policy. Previously, Dr. Cook was a Research Fellow at the Brookings Institution and a Soref Research Fellow at the Washington Institute for Near East Policy.

Larry J. Diamond is a Senior Fellow at the Hoover Institution and Professor of Political Science and Sociology at Stanford University, as well as Co-Editor of the *Journal of Democracy* and Co-Director of the International Forum for Democratic Studies at the National Endowment for Democracy. Dr. Diamond was a Senior Adviser on political transition to the Coalition Provisional Authority in Baghdad from January to March 2004.

Michele D. Dunne* is Editor of the *Arab Reform Bulletin* at the Carnegie Endowment for International Peace and Visiting Assistant Professor of Arabic at Georgetown University. She is a former Middle East specialist in the U.S. Department of State and served in assignments at the National Security Council, the U.S. Embassy in Cairo, the Secretary of State's Policy Planning Staff, the National Intelligence Council, and the U.S. Consulate General in Jerusalem.

Noah Feldman is Assistant Professor of Law at New York University. He recently returned from Baghdad, where he served as Senior Adviser to the Coalition Provisional Authority on the new Iraqi constitutional process. He is the author of, most recently, *After Jihad: America and the Struggle for Islamic Democracy*.

F. Gregory Gause III* is Associate Professor of Political Science at the University of Vermont and Director of the University's Middle East Studies Program. Previously, he served on the faculty of Columbia

University and as a Fellow for Arab and Islamic studies at the Council on Foreign Relations. He is the author of *Oil Monarchies: Domestic and Security Challenges in the Arab Gulf States*, along with other articles and monographs on the politics of the Middle East.

Amy W. Hawthorne is an independent consultant specializing in Arab politics and democracy promotion. She provides strategic, analytical, and program-management expertise to U.S. and Arab organizations working to promote democratic change in the Middle East. Previously, she was an Associate in the Democracy and Rule of Law Project at the Carnegie Endowment for International Peace, where she served as the founding Editor of the endowment's *Arab Reform Bulletin*. She was also previously Senior Program Officer for the Middle East at the International Foundation for Election Systems, a Washington-based democracy-promotion organization, where she designed and managed projects to promote governance and political participation in several Arab countries, and a Fulbright scholar in Egypt.

Robert J. Katz is Senior Director at the Goldman Sachs Group, Inc. Previously, Mr. Katz was General Counsel and Partner at Goldman Sachs and, prior to that, Partner at Sullivan & Cromwell in New York City. He currently serves as Chair of the Board of Trustees of Horace Mann School and as a Trustee of Cornell University, a member of the Dean's Advisory Board of Harvard Law School, and a Director of the Survivors of the Shoah Visual History Foundation.

Mel Levine is Partner in the Los Angeles and Washington, DC, offices of Gibson Dunn & Crutcher, LLP, and served in the U.S. Congress from 1983 to 1993. Mr. Levine previously served as the U.S. Chair of the U.S.-Israeli-Palestinian "Anti-incitement" Committee established by the Wye Plantation peace agreement. He is a Trustee of the University of California (Berkeley) Foundation, a former Trustee of the United States Holocaust Museum, and a Director of the Pacific Council on International Policy.

Abdeslam E. Maghraoui is Associate Director of the Research and Studies Program of the Muslim World Initiative at the United States

Institute of Peace. He was most recently a Visiting Lecturer and Resident Scholar in Princeton University's Department of Politics. Previously, Dr. Maghraoui served as Director of al-Madina, a nonprofit organization dedicated to promoting accountable governance in the Arab world.

Joshua Muravchik is a Resident Scholar at the American Enterprise Institute for Public Policy Research. He is also an Adjunct Professor at the World Politics Institute and an Adjunct Scholar at the Washington Institute for Near East Policy. Dr. Muravchik serves on the Editorial Boards of *World Affairs* and the *Journal of Democracy*.

Michael N. Pocalyko* is Managing Director and Chief Executive Officer of Monticello Capital, an investment bank in Reston, Virginia, and New York. He also chairs Erdevel Europa S.à r.l., a global corporation headquartered in Luxembourg that, as a private venture, he formed to build water infrastructure in Saudi Arabia and throughout the Middle East. He was a Naval aviator who commanded multinational operations in Beirut and the Persian Gulf and has served in both federal and Virginia government. Mr. Pocalyko is an active corporate director in high-technology industries and a Trustee of Fairleigh Dickinson University in New Jersey.

William A. Rugh* is currently an independent consultant. He was most recently President and Chief Executive Officer of AMIDEAST. A Foreign Service veteran, he served as U.S. Ambassador to the Republic of Yemen and to the United Arab Emirates.

Anita Sharma is the Information Officer for the International Organization for Migration's (IOM) Tsunami Emergency Relief Program in Indonesia. Previously, she directed the Conflict Prevention Project at the Woodrow Wilson International Center for Scholars. She was a foreign policy adviser for the 2004 Kerry-Edwards presidential campaign. She also worked with IOM in Iraq, Jordan, and Kuwait and served as an Elections Observer and Supervisor for Kosovo elections in 2001 and 2002 with the Organization for Security and Cooperation in Europe and the Council of Europe. Ms. Sharma has also served in research positions at the Carnegie Commission on Preventing Deadly Conflict and the Association of the United States Army. She is a term member of the Council on Foreign Relations and a member of Women in International Security (WIIS).

George Vradenburg III is President of the Vradenburg Foundation. He was most recently Strategic Adviser and Executive Vice President for Global and Strategy Policy at AOL Time Warner. Prior to joining AOL Time Warner, Mr. Vradenburg served as Senior Vice President and General Counsel of CBS, and as Executive Vice President at Fox. Mr. Vradenburg is currently Co-Chair of the Potomac Conference Task Force on Emergency Preparedness for the Greater Washington Region.

Vin Weber is Co-Chair of the Task Force and Managing Partner of the Washington office of Clark & Weinstock. He is also Chairman of the National Endowment for Democracy. Previously, Mr. Weber was President of Empower America. He served in the U.S. House of Representatives from 1981 to 1993 representing Minnesota.

Tamara Cofman Wittes is Research Fellow in the Saban Center for Middle East Policy at the Brookings Institution, where she is completing a book on U.S. democracy promotion in the Arab world. Previously, Dr. Wittes served as Middle East Specialist at the United States Institute of Peace, Director of Programs at the Middle East Institute, and Adjunct Professor of Security Studies at Georgetown University. She is the Editor of *How Israelis and Palestinians Negotiate: A Cross-Cultural Analysis of the Oslo Peace Process*.

Tarik M. Yousef is Assistant Professor of Economics in the School of Foreign Service and Shaykh al-Sabah Chair in Arab Studies in the Center for Contemporary Arab Studies at Georgetown University. He is also a consultant on the Middle East and North Africa region for the World Bank and the UN Millennium Project. He worked as an Economist for the International Monetary Fund from 1997 to 1999. Dr. Yousef specializes in development economics and economic history with a particular focus on the Middle East.

Task Force Observers

Rachel Bronson
Council on Foreign Relations

Craig Charney
Charney Research

Isobel Coleman
Council on Foreign Relations

Zachary Karabell
Fred Alger Management

Judith Kipper
Council on Foreign Relations

Elliot J. Schrage
Council on Foreign Relations

Ray Takeyh
Council on Foreign Relations

Mary Anne Weaver
Council on Foreign Relations

William Woodward
The Albright Group LLC

Appendixes

APPENDIX A

Major Islamist Movements in the Middle East

Country	Organization	Year Established	Current Use of Violence	Political Participation
Algeria	Islamic Salvation Front	1989	No	No
	Armed Islamic Group	1993	Yes	No
	Salafist Group for Preaching and Combat	1996	Yes	No
Bahrain	Islamic Action Society	2002	No	No
	The Islamic Pulpit	2002	No	Yes
	Harmony	1994	No	No
Egypt	Muslim Brotherhood	1928	No	No
	Hizb al-Wasat	1995	No	No
Iraq	United Iraqi Alliance	2004	No	Yes
	Iraqi Islamic Party	1960	No	Yes
	Supreme Council for Islamic Revolution in Iraq	1982	Yes	Yes
	Ansar al-Islam	2001	Yes	No
	Unity and Jihad Group	Late 1990s	Yes	No
	Association of Muslim Scholars	2003	No	No
	Islamic Call Party	1957	No	Yes
	The Mahdi Army	2003	Yes	Yes
Jordan	Muslim Brotherhood/Islamic Action Front	1945	No	Yes
	Al-Qaeda	Late 1990s	Yes	No

(continued on next page)

59

Appendix A *(continued)*

Country	Organization	Year Established	Current Use of Violence	Political Partici- pation
Kuwait	Islamic National Alliance	1989	No	Yes
	Islamic Constitutional Movement	1991	No	Yes
	Islamic Popular Alliance	Mid-1970s	No	Yes
Lebanon	League of Followers	Early 1990s	Yes	No
	Amal/Lebanese Resistance Battalions	1975	No	Yes
	Hizballah	1979	Yes	Yes
Morocco	Justice and Development	1997	No	Yes
	Justice and Charity	1985	No	No
	Salafi Jihadi/Al-Qaeda	Early 1990s	Yes	No
Saudi Arabia	Movement for Islamic Reform in Arabia	1996	No	No
	Shi'a Reform Movement	1975	No	No
	Committee for the Defense of Legitimate Rights	1993	No	No
	Al-Qaeda in the Arabian Peninsula	Mid-1990s	Yes	No
Sudan	National Islamic Front	1989	No	Yes
	Umma Party	1945	No	No
	Popular National Congress	2000	No	No
Tunisia	Renaissance Party	1989	No	No
West Bank and Gaza	Islamic Jihad	1981	Yes	No
	Hamas	1987	Yes	Yes
Yemen	Al-Qaeda/Islamic Army of Aden-Abyan	1997	Yes	No
	Believing Youth	2004	Yes	No
	Reform Party	1991	No	Yes

Primary Macroeconomic Indicators

Country	Gross National Income (GNI) (Current U.S. $b)	GNI per Capita (Current U.S. $)	Gross Domestic Product (GDP) (Current U.S. $b)	Annual GDP Growth (percent)	Goods and Services Exports (percent of GDP)	Imports (percent of GDP)	Gross Capital Formation (percent of GDP)
Algeria (2003)	61.6	1,930	66.5	6.8	39.0	24.3	30.0
Bahrain (2002)	71.6	10,850	7.7	5.1	81.1	65.0	17.5
Egypt (2003)	93.9	1,390	82.4	3.2	21.7	23.6	17.1
Jordan (2003)	9.8	1,850	9.9	3.2	44.5	70.1	22.7
Kuwait (2003)	43.0	17,960	41.7	9.9	48.3 (2002)	39.6 (2002)	9.1 (2002)
Lebanon (2003)	18.2	4,040	19.0	2.7	13.4	39.0	16.7
Libya (2002)	N/A	N/A	19.1	N/A	47.9	36.5	14.1
Morocco (2003)	39.4	1,310	43.7	5.2	32.3	36.4	23.8
Oman (2002)	19.9	7,830	20.3	0.0	56.8	35.5	12.8
Saudi Arabia (2003)	208.1	9,240	214.7	7.2	46.9	24.1	19.4

(continued on next page)

Appendix B *(continued)*

Country	Gross National Income (GNI) (Current U.S. $b)	GNI per Capita (Current U.S. $)	Gross Domestic Product (GDP) (Current U.S. $b)	Annual GDP Growth (percent)	Goods and Services		Gross Capital Formation (percent of GDP)
					Exports (percent of GDP)	Imports (percent of GDP)	
Sudan (2003)	15.4	460	17.8	6.0	16.3	12.1	20.5
Syria (2003)	20.2	1,160	21.5	2.5	40.2	33.0	23.6
Tunisia (2003)	22.2	2,240	25.0	5.6	43.1	47.2	25.1
West Bank and Gaza (2003)	3.7	1,110	3.5	− 1.7	10.0	49.0	2.5
United Arab Emirates (2002)	N/A	N/A	71.0	1.8	N/A	N/A	N/A
Yemen (2003)	9.9	520	10.8	3.8	31.2	35.9	17.1

SOURCE: World Development Indicators Database Online, April 2005.

APPENDIX C

Data on the Information Technology Sector

Personal Computers	
Country	Per 1,000 People (2002)
Algeria	7.7
Egypt	16.6
Iraq	8.3
Jordan	37.5
Lebanon	80.5
Libya	23.4
Morocco	23.6
Oman	35.0
Saudi Arabia	130.2
Sudan	6.1
Syria	19.4
Tunisia	30.7
United Arab Emirates	129.0
West Bank and Gaza	36.2
Yemen	7.4
Middle East and North Africa Region	38.2

(continued on next page)

Appendix C *(continued)*

	Internet Usage			
Country	Users per 1,000 People (2002)	Cost of 20 Hours Usage (U.S. $) (2003)	Expenditures on IT as a Percentage of Monthly Gross National Income Per Capita (2003)	Number of Secure Servers (2003)
Algeria	16	18	12.4	4
Egypt	28	5	4.5	17
Iraq	1	N/A	N/A	N/A
Jordan	58	26	18.0	9
Lebanon	117	37	11.1	16
Libya	23	19	3.8	N/A
Morocco	24	25	25.5	15
Oman	66	24	3.8	1
Saudi Arabia	62	35	4.9	26
Sudan	3	161	550.8	N/A
Syria	13	55	58.6	1
Tunisia	52	17	10.4	13
United Arab Emirates	337	13	0.8	83
West Bank and Gaza	30	25	32.8	N/A
Yemen	5	31	75.3	1
Middle East and North Africa Region	37	31	29.9	103

SOURCE: International Telecommunication Union, *World Telecommunication Development Report 2003: Access Indicators for the Information Society*, 7th edition, 2003.

APPENDIX D

Information on Qualified Industrial Zones

The formation of qualified industrial zones (QIZs) is permissible under a 1996 congressional amendment to the United States International Free Trade Agreement authorizing the executive branch to allow Egypt and Jordan to export products to the United States duty-free, as long as they contain Israeli inputs. In order to qualify as a QIZ, designated industrial parks must encompass portions of Israel and either Egypt or Jordan, although such zones do not necessarily need to be contiguous. This allows for the establishment of individual zones in specific states. Under the 1999 QIZ agreement with Jordan, all products eligible for duty-free export to the United States must contain a minimum of 11.7 percent value added in a Jordanian QIZ, 8 percent value added in Israel, and an additional 15.3 percent value added from either a Jordanian QIZ, Israel, the West Bank, or the Gaza Strip. A similar agreement signed with Egypt in December 2004 likewise requires QIZ factories to provide 35 percent of total inputs, except Egypt and Israel are each required to contribute a minimum of 11.7 percent of value added. Since 1999, the U.S. Trade Representative (USTR), in consultation with the Jordanian government, has established thirteen QIZs in Jordan, providing more than 35,000 jobs and attracting between $85 million and $100 million in direct investment. Under the direction of the executive branch and in accordance with Israel and Egypt, the USTR has approved the establishment of three Egyptian QIZs in Cairo, Alexandria, and Suez.

APPENDIX E
Major Arab Satellite Television Networks

Network	Broadcast from	Year Launched	Content
Al-Arabiyya	United Arab Emirates (UAE)	2003	News
Lebanese Broadcasting Center (LBC)	Lebanon	2001	News/Entertainment
Al-Ikhbariyya	Saudi Arabia	2003	News
Al-Jazeera	Qatar	1996	News
Al-Manar	Lebanon	2000	News/Entertainment/Religious
Abu Dhabi Television	UAE	2000	News/Entertainment/Business
Arab Radio and Television (ART)	Italy	1994	News/Entertainment/Religious
Egyptian Radio and Television	Egypt	1990	News/Culture/Entertainment
Dubai Television	UAE	2000	News/Entertainment/Business
Future Television	Lebanon	1993	News/Entertainment
Dream T.V.	Egypt	2001	Culture/Entertainment

(continued on next page)

Appendix E *(continued)*

Network	Broadcast from	Year Launched	Content
Jordanian Radio and Television Corporation	Jordan	1993	News/Culture/Entertainment
Kuwait Television	Kuwait	1991	News/Entertainment
Middle East Broadcasting Center (MBC)	UAE	1991	News/Entertainment/Business
National Broadcasting Network (NBN)	Lebanon	1996	News
New Television	Lebanon	2001	News/Entertainment
Orbit Television	Saudi Arabia	1994	News/Entertainment/Sports
Nile T.V.	Egypt	1993	News/Entertainment/Foreign Language

APPENDIX F

Middle East Partnership Initiative Spending

	Total Appropriated Funds (FY 2002–FY 2005)				
	FY02	**FY03**	**FY04**	**FY05**	Total
MEPI	$29,000,000	$100,000,000	$45,000,000	$90,000,000	**$264,000,000**
AID Democracy & Governance					**$797,966,000**
Egypt	9,420,000	13,300,000	37,050,000	30,100,000*	
Iraq	0	174,611,000	388,000,000	0*	
Jordan	0	0	32,850,000	40,000,000*	
Lebanon	7,000,000	5,000,000	4,000,000	7,000,000*	
Morocco	0	0	0	4,000,000*	
West Bank and Gaza	11,375,000	10,150,000	13,350,000	7,500,000*	
Yemen	0	400,000	680,000	2,180,000*	
Total					**$1,061,966,000**

*Indicates amount requested; actual country totals for FY05 not available by press time. Prepared by Tamara Cofman Wittes of the Saban Center for Middle East Policy at the Brookings Institution.

Appendix F *(continued)*

Pillar	MEPI Spending by Program Pillar (December 2002–November 2004)			
	FY02	FY03	Total	% Change
Economic	$6,134,425	$18,491,855	**$24,626,280**	301
Education	4,000,000	21,900,000	**$25,900,000**	548
Political	10,500,000	23,515,000	**$34,015,000**	224
Women's	6,036,000	10,945,904	**$16,981,904**	181
Other (MEPI Small Grants)		1,700,000	**$1,700,000**	N/A
Total	**$26,670,425**	**$76,552,759**	**$103,223,184**	287

SOURCE: Tamara Cofman Wittes and Sarah Yerkes, "The Middle East Partnership Initiative: Progress, Problems, and Prospects," Middle East Memo No. 5 (Washington: Saban Center for Middle East Policy at the Brookings Institution, November 29, 2004).

Selected Reports of Independent Task Forces Sponsored by the Council on Foreign Relations

*†*Building a North American Community* (2005), John P. Manley, Pedro Aspe, and William F. Weld, Co-Chairs; Thomas P. d'Aquino, Andrés Rozental, and Robert A. Pastor, Vice Chairs; Chappell H. Lawson, Project Director

*†*Iran: Time for a New Approach* (2004), Zbigniew Brzezinski and Robert Gates, Co-Chairs; Suzanne Maloney, Project Director

*†*Renewing the Atlantic Partnership* (2004), Henry A. Kissinger and Lawrence H. Summers, Co-Chairs; Charles A. Kupchan, Project Director

*†*Nonlethal Weapons and Capabilities* (2004), Graham T. Allison and Paul X. Kelley, Co-Chairs; Richard L. Garwin, Project Director

*†*New Priorities in South Asia: U.S. Policy Toward India, Pakistan, and Afghanistan* (2003), Frank G.Wisner II, Nicholas Platt, and Marshall M. Bouton, Co-Chairs; Dennis Kux and Mahnaz Ispahani, Project Co-Directors; Cosponsored with the Asia Society

*†*Finding America's Voice: A Strategy for Reinvigorating U.S. Public Diplomacy* (2003), Peter G. Peterson, Chair; Jennifer Sieg, Project Director

*†*Emergency Responders:Drastically Underfunded, Dangerously Unprepared* (2003), Warren B. Rudman, Chair; Richard A. Clarke, Senior Adviser; Jamie F. Metzl, Project Director

*†*Burma:Time for Change* (2003), Mathea Falco, Chair

*†*Meeting the North Korean Nuclear Challenge* (2003), Morton I. Abramowitz and James T. Laney, Co-Chairs; Eric Heginbotham, Project Director

*†*Chinese Military Power* (2003), Harold Brown, Chair; Joseph W. Prueher, Vice Chair; Adam Segal, Project Director

*†*Iraq: The Day After* (2003), Thomas R. Pickering and James R. Schlesinger, Co-Chairs; Eric P. Schwartz, Project Director

*†*Threats to Democracy* (2002), Madeleine K. Albright and Bronislaw Geremek, Co-Chairs; Morton H. Halperin, Project Director; Elizabeth Frawley Bagley, Associate Director

*†*America-Still Unprepared, Still in Danger* (2002), Gary Hart and Warren B. Rudman, Co-Chairs; Stephen Flynn, Project Director

*†*Terrorist Financing* (2002), Maurice R. Greenberg, Chair;William F.Wechsler and Lee S.Wolosky, Project Co-Directors

*†*Enhancing U.S. Leadership at the United Nations* (2002), David Dreier and Lee H. Hamilton, Co-Chairs; Lee Feinstein and Adrian Karatnycky, Project Co-Directors

*†*Testing North Korea: The Next Stage in U.S. and ROK Policy* (2001), Morton I. Abramowitz and James T. Laney, Co-Chairs; Robert A. Manning, Project Director

*†*The United States and Southeast Asia: A Policy Agenda for the New Administration* (2001), J. Robert Kerrey, Chair; Robert A. Manning, Project Director

*†*Strategic Energy Policy: Challenges for the 21st Century* (2001), Edward L. Morse, Chair; Amy Myers Jaffe, Project Director

*†*State Department Reform* (2001), Frank C. Carlucci, Chair; Ian J. Brzezinski, Project Coordinator; Cosponsored with the Center for Strategic and International Studies

*†*U.S.-Cuban Relations in the 21st Century: A Follow-on-Report* (2001), Bernard W. Aronson and William D. Rogers, Co-Chairs; Julia Sweig and Walter Mead, Project Directors

*†*A Letter to the President and a Memorandum on U.S. Policy Toward Brazil* (2001), Stephen Robert, Chair; Kenneth Maxwell, Project Director

*†*Toward Greater Peace and Security in Colombia* (2000), Bob Graham and Brent Scowcroft, Co-Chairs; Michael Shifter, Project Director; Cosponsored with the Inter-American Dialogue

---

†Available on the Council on Foreign Relations website at www.cfr.org.
*Available from Brookings Institution Press. To order, call 800-275-1447.